Making a DIFFERENCE

Also by Dean Gualco

What Happened to the American Dream?

The Meaning of Life

The Great People of Our Time

The Good Manager: A Guide for the 21st Century Manager

*Choices and Consequences: The Disintegrating Political,
Economic, and Societal Institutions of the United States*

Making a DIFFERENCE

Changing the World in Which You Live

Dean Gualco

iUniverse LLC
Bloomington

MAKING A DIFFERENCE
CHANGING THE WORLD IN WHICH YOU LIVE

iUniverse books may be ordered through booksellers or by contacting:

iUniverse LLC
1663 Liberty Drive
Bloomington, IN 47403
www.iuniverse.com
1-800-Authors (1-800-288-4677)

Because of the dynamic nature of the Internet, any web addresses or links contained in this book may have changed since publication and may no longer be valid. The views expressed in this work are solely those of the author and do not necessarily reflect the views of the publisher, and the publisher hereby disclaims any responsibility for them.

Any people depicted in stock imagery provided by Thinkstock are models, and such images are being used for illustrative purposes only. Certain stock imagery © Thinkstock.

ISBN: 978-1-4917-1287-0 (sc)
ISBN: 978-1-4917-1289-4 (hc)
ISBN: 978-1-4917-1288-7 (e)

Library of Congress Control Number: 2013919696

Printed in the United States of America.

iUniverse rev. date: 10/29/2013

To my children, Gunner and Toria,

who have given me a blessed life.

Always look for the good along the road of life.

To make a difference, you must change the world;

to change the world, you must change yourself.

CONTENTS

Acknowledgments ix

Introduction xiii

Chapter 1   Foundations of Change 1

Chapter 2   Reasons to Change 11

Chapter 3   The Conditions for Change. 23

Chapter 4   The Definitive Change Process 39

Chapter 5   The Change Agent 53

Chapter 6   The Realms of Change 65

Chapter 7   Three Ds and Two Cs 85

Chapter 8   The Great Changes for Our Age. 95

Appendix 103

Acknowledgments

I would like to extend my gratitude and appreciation to the following people, without whom I would not be the man I am today.

- The Man Upstairs, who has made this all possible.

- My parents, who have provided shining examples of how to live a decent and honorable life.

- My buddy of more than thirty years, Bill Munroe. Friends come and go, but there always seem to be one or two who last a lifetime.

- Jeff Thompson, who I describe to just about anyone as the epitome of a great guy. We should all be so lucky to become that kind of person.

- John Ellis, the godfather to my children. Whether playing golf or having dinner with him and his wife, "I hope everyone meets a John Ellis in their life."

- Thanks to Sierra Brucia, "genuinely one of the good guys in life . . . Go Colts!"

- Keith Williams, the first real friend I ever had.

- To my childhood buddy from St. Bernard's Grammar School, Jon Smith, who was killed by a drunk driver his freshman year in college. His death constantly reminds me to "do something" worthwhile with my time since his was cut so tragically short.

- And, of course, my kids Gunner and Toria, who have given me a blessed life.

This country has progressed and its people prospered

because all shared the principles of its shared culture:

that you obey the laws and pay your taxes,

that you are a kind and honorable person,

that you work hard and keep most of what you earn,

that you share with the less fortunate,

and that you strive to make the world a better place.

That belief seems to have frayed over the past decades,

but it can be changed.

Introduction

Changing an organization. Changing a culture. Changing a country. Realizing your ambitions, controlling your fate, and achieving unrivaled greatness is derived from knowing what to change, how to change, and, most importantly, why to change. The lessons and stories in this book provide the knowledge and inspiration to change your life and to help change the world along the way.

Defining change can be challenging for some; understanding change can be mystifying for most. Simply defined, change is doing something different—it can be anything from trying an unusual recipe to traveling to a foreign country or meeting a new friend. These changes are oftentimes beyond the comfort and security of an orderly life. Being apprehensive about a new experience is natural and even expected, but exhilaration often follows.

Change is mystifying because there is not a systematic, prescribed format to study what to change, when to change, and how to change. Moreover, the impact and consequences of change cannot often be predicted with a high degree of confidence, which can lead to rising instability and insecurity. That said, a broader understanding of change can be realized and a greater awareness of its challenges and complexities gained by learning the eight key concepts of change. They are:

1. The impetus to change is determined by asking one simple question: Can a better life be achieved by traveling the same road or by choosing a different path? Rarely is the better life achieved by following the same path.

2. Change is part of life. The insatiable quest to think, be, act, and behave differently from our parents, siblings, schoolmates, friends, and neighbors pervades and consumes our culture.

3. Change can be learned. Reading voraciously, studying the perils of complacency and the thrills of adventure, knowing where to go, and striving for greatness provide the knowledge and skills to triumph through change.

4. Avoiding or hindering change seldom results in a steadier and stabler present, but rather a more unpredictable and unstable future.

5. Change viewed as beneficial is always welcome and supported; change viewed as harmful is always unwelcome and resisted.

6. Change favors those who can adapt to the changing circumstances of a different future.

7. Those with natural curiosity—the explorers and inventors who think differently—rule the world. Imagination and originality are the defining characteristics of healthy organizations and wealthy employees.

8. Never be a victim of change. Accept responsibility for your life, control the trajectory of its course, and determine your own destiny. Change may be inevitable, but failure is not.

We live in an increasingly volatile and precarious time in which we must renew our country, transform our culture, innovate our organizations, retrain our employees, and better ourselves. We must change a world where violence is favored rather than peace, deflecting blame rather than assuming responsibility, leveling criticism rather than unstinting praise, and instilling fear rather than offering hope. Finally, our financial systems must be restored, the environment must be repaired, diseases must be eradicated, famine must be ended, and political structures must be rebuilt. It is a world dangerously close to the precipice.

Though we do dream of something better, and those dreams of a better world may be worthwhile, they are worthless unless we do something about them. Fortunately, our history has not yet been written, nor has our destiny been determined. We are limited only by our dreams of a better world and our determination to make a difference.

Too often, we believe the major problems of our age are caused by others. The major problems start and end with each and every one of us. Changing others and the world begins by changing ourselves. My eternal hope is that by reading this book, you will work to become a more decent and honorable person, one who takes responsibility for your actions; works to rebuild, not destroy, the earth and its inhabitants; and seeks to be more appreciative of your good fortune and more giving to those less fortunate. If you can take that opportunity, you will make a difference in the lives of your fellow man and forever change the world in which you live.

> We are limited only by our dreams of a better world and our determination to make a difference.

CHAPTER 1

Foundations of Change

Doctors study medicine, attorneys study the law, and accountants study the tax code. To gain a better understanding of chemistry, economics, or linguistics, students learn the philosophies and theories that serve as the foundation of that discipline. Education forms the basis for effective decision making, and those who are destined to change the world or change an organization must diligently study the foundations associated with change.

There are several philosophies and concepts that form the foundation of change. A greater and broader understanding of these concepts allows one to better prepare for; learn about; and master how to change, when to change, what to change, and why to change. These concepts are:

- Change is remarkable yet destabilizing. Whether curing polio or establishing the Internet, change effects society.

- Change must be viewed as advantageous and to be welcomed. Change viewed as such will almost always be enthusiastically sought and promoted.

- Change favors those in control of their future. Those in control of their destiny are more likely to be the victors, not the victims, of change.

- Change favors those who can adapt to a different future. Those who can adapt to change are more likely to profit and overcome from its ramifications.

- In nearly every instance, change offers the chance for a better life. Fewer circumstances hold the promise of a better life than the ability to change the present.

Change is remarkable yet destabilizing
For all the great that has come from change, it is surprising—even astounding—that change is nearly universally rebutted, refuted, and resisted. Hundreds of millions were freed from the shackles of communism, tens of millions were freed from the oppressive regimes in Afghanistan and Iraq, and millions were freed from the totalitarian

regimes in Libya and Tunisia. Generations were saved by the discoveries of penicillin and the polio vaccine, and the elderly live far healthier and more productive lives because of the advances in medicine and medical technology. Advances in technology have created untold opportunities for employment throughout the world, whether in India, China, South Africa, or Poland. Rarely in history have employment opportunities been as broad and plentiful for those choosing to sacrifice and work hard, have medical advances been as astonishing, and has freedom been as universally shared and enjoyed.

Too often, though, change is viewed through the prism of conflict and negativity. We do live in remarkable times, but we are encapsulated in a similarly destabilizing time. The military overthrow of the Egyptian government, the devastating rise in spending and fall in productivity in Greece, the corruption that pervades many countries on the African continent, and the sinking employment opportunities in the United States are prominent examples. We have witnessed millions lose their jobs through changing technology and communications, countless lose their health and retirement benefits through rampant cost-cutting as organizations try to compete with new entrants into the global marketplace, and thousands lose their homes through foreclosure as they are unable to pay their mortgage and other basic expenses. The old are unable to retire, while the young are unable to find jobs.

Such is the nature of change and its profound impact on the physical, emotional, and social lives of the world's inhabitants.

Simultaneously, morphing social mores are seen to undermine our faith in community and weaken the bonds within our family and friends. Divorce seems to be more commonplace, and single-parent families are becoming more the norm than the exception. Some of these circumstances did not exist decades ago, yet these events have become representative of the destructive repercussions of a changing world, symbolic of a fast-paced age that decimates the hopes and dreams of far too many. No matter the advances achieved, there are those left behind who lament a time more favorable, and its return more advantageous.

Like death and taxes, change is a certainty in life. However, over the past half century, change has progressed at a pace unrivaled in our history. Never before has change advanced so rapidly and continuously as it has during the second half of the twentieth century. The transition from an agrarian to industrial society occurred over a century, while the transition from laptops to tablets occurred, it seemed, over a few years. Cameras and Kodak film ruled the picture business for more than a century, yet the dominance of digital cameras lasted less than a decade before smartphones made carrying a camera unnecessary for many. State and city maps were a staple of the summer vacation for decades, a circumstance made irrelevant with the advent of handheld GPS devices. They generated millions annually, but their dominance lasted less than a decade as iPhones and Android phones offered free mobile applications similar to GPS devices. GPS device sales plummeted, and as the GPS device made handheld maps obsolete, so too shortly thereafter did iPhones and Android phones make the GPS device obsolete. Change forced the handheld GPS devices onto the scrap heap of technology, a place littered with once grand products.

Whereas the time frame for previous generations to relearn, retool, and retrain according to the new methods and technologies lasted years or even decades, the time frame for today's generation seems to be measured in months. This fact has led to a rising tide of insecurity and instability felt by so many today. This segment of the population mistakenly targets its anger at the negative consequences of change rather than its positive results such as better health care, a cleaner environment, and a recognition that fairness and equality should be hallmarks of a progressive society.

Though it bewilders some and invigorates others, we live in a remarkable era. Progress has cured many diseases and fed millions of people, and there is still more that can be done. Ironically, change is a greater force for stability than inability, and its welcome occurrence has led to a better standard of living, not worse, for most of the world's population.

Change must be viewed as advantageous and to be welcomed
The degree of acceptance or resistance to change is almost solely related to how much people perceive they will benefit from the change. Few resist

a medication change that alleviates discomfort, a performance evaluation that results in a pay increase, the installation of airbags that drastically reduces injury and the risk of death in an accident, the generation of solar power that reduces our carbon footprint, or the passage of a new telecommuting policy that allows you to work from home. Few resist the change that results in a new car, free vacations, new promotions, higher salary, bigger homes, better friends, lottery winnings, or greater longevity. Though these changes can have profound impacts on one's life, they are welcome changes because one's interests are advanced, regardless of the level of control one has over the change itself.

As we have learned, change—whether expected or unexpected, planned or unplanned—is not the force of destruction that so many expect and believe. At its most basic, it is a change in circumstances, and the consequences of those circumstances are a determining factor in how one responds to change. The degree of resistance to change is nearly wholly determined by the ability of the changer to convey the personal benefit the changee would receive from the change. Change must be framed as a benefit to those involved. Layoffs in one area of an organization must be seen as necessary to benefit the remaining areas of the organization. Higher taxes are universally resisted unless they can be shown to benefit the public. The closure of a public school is fought unless residents believe monies can be diverted to remaining schools to raise scholastic possibilities and achievements.

The notion that change is resisted because it is different or that most people resist change is simply untrue. Most resist change because the consequences of the change are not advantageous. Thus, for change to be heartedly welcomed, gratefully accepted, and collaboratively implemented, it must be seen as advantageous to those affected or impacted.

Change favors those in control of their future
At its core, change is about doing something different: creating a different product, service, vision, organization, process, or person. It is about planning to do something tomorrow different from what has been done today or doing something today different from what was done yesterday. It is altering the manner in which someone thinks,

believes, acts, and behaves. It is changing ambitions and desires, hopes and dreams, and the destiny that one hopes to realize.

Too many believe that they are powerless to stop the storms of change. Not many welcome the opportunity to be powerless to determine their own future and fate. Even fewer welcome the opportunity of being dictated to or being dominated by happenstance and circumstance. Throughout history, millions of citizens have rebelled against the powerful and the dominating, demanding more control over their future than subservience to others.

Most want the ability to control their future, and change that affects this ability is nearly universally opposed and resisted. They see themselves as victims of circumstances, as if they are buoys marking the waves of a thunderous ocean. Nothing can be done to slow the rising tide or tame the currents that slam into the buoys, and they are therefore pounded by events beyond their control.

Bell buoys are stationary, sedentary blocks without direction. They exist to occupy a space and perform a singular task, even if that task is no longer needed or valued. The waters may rise or fall or move fast or slow, but the buoy remains committed to its mission. They are rudderless objects in a vast ocean, performing a task that scarcely has any value as the waves crash against this seemingly worthless object.

The bell buoy exists to perform a singular task that is beneficial to very few. It neither moves nor responds to the often-vicious pounding of the sea. That, though, is by design. It is undeterred in performing its function, no matter the repercussions. As such, the bell buoy is required to perform its task regardless of the damage done, which most certainly will occur.

While bell buoys exert little control over their station in life, the same cannot be said for most people. Most have control over the type of company for which they work, the type of clubs they choose to join, the type of debts they assume, and the type of income they make. They have control over the type of person they marry, the type of friends they make, and the very type of person they endeavor to become. Each choice reflects a degree of control you have over your future, regardless of whether you choose to exercise that right.

You can be the catalyst for change or the consequence of change. Too many fail to choose the right path in life and therefore become victims of their own poor choices. They have relinquished their responsibility to choose their own path in life and determine their own fate. They are not victims of change they cannot control; they are victims of poor professional and personal choices and have become susceptible to the winds of a changing world.

Those most disadvantaged by change are those who have abdicated control to make their own decisions and choose their own path for their future. By doing so, they have been the victim, by choice, of a future they are now powerless to control.

Change favors those who can adapt to a different future
All too regularly, change is miscast, misguided, and miscommunicated. Employees are told they must do more with less, but not often told it is because the organization wants to expand funding for research and development efforts. Employees are told the number of employees must be reduced and compensation reconfigured, but not told it is so the organization can better compete against low-wage countries throughout the world. These organizations that take the often-difficult and treacherous opportunity to change their very operations (to rethink, retool, and refocus their operations and cultures) are creating organizations designed to better compete in an increasingly complex business environment, take advantage of changing circumstances, and morph with the age and stand the test of time.

These changes offer the best chance for the long-term viability of the organization and those who serve it. But there is a price to pay, and for some, it is heady. Reduced employment opportunities, diminished promotional prospects, falling salaries, and diminishing benefits are the price to pay for some, while continued employment and a higher income are the rewards for others. Change does not determine the winners and losers. Rather, it is a person's ability to adapt to change that may be the defining characteristic of those who are advantaged and disadvantaged by change.

We have greater control over our lives than it might seem, and in those scarce occasions where we seemingly have little control over events in our life, we do have the ability to adapt to that new future if we choose to exercise that right. We may not be able to choose the new supervisors or managers of our organization, but we can adapt to their different personalities, styles, and ambitions. We may not be able to understand the latest cellular technology (with its growing applications and complexities), but we can adapt to its use. We may be affected by the movement from a manufacturing-based economy to a service-based economy, but we can adapt to the new workplace by returning to school and gaining broader knowledge and skills that increase our chances of future employability. In general, a changing world is a better world, though some are destined not to benefit—at least initially.

Sadly, adaptation is terribly difficult. Personal insecurities and jealousies hinder our ability to adapt to changing cultures and mores, destroying even the strongest relationships. Fewer marriages survive, and few friendships last a lifetime. Times change, and the inability or unwillingness to adapt causes the destruction of the very relationships necessary during turbulent times.

However, adaptation does not mean abandonment. We should never abandon those values and goodness that are the very essence of who we are and what we stand for. We should never turn toward incivility if incivility is rewarded or animosity if that destructive trait becomes the prevailing characteristic of a group or organization. We can adapt our knowledge, skills, perceptions, and understandings. We cannot, however, abandon our sense of right or wrong, hate or love, and good or bad.

As we progress through life, there are occasions where change must be resisted and a future must not be experienced. We should not adapt to the new supervisor who is morally challenged and ethically corrupt, whose only happiness comes from the denigration of his or her employees (a circumstance I have experienced). Nor should we adapt to the rudeness of our children because that is the socially acceptable culture of their generation. We must stand firm and never abandon the noble and decent values ingrained in a good person, but be willing to adapt where adaptation does not conflict with a fair and just society.

The ability to adapt to an unknown and more complex future benefits those who are ambitious, energetic, and confident, traits that are emblematic of a person who thinks, believes, acts, and behaves differently. While one may not have the ability to control or benefit from the future, one does have the ability to adapt to it, and it is this adaptation that determines the happiness or sadness and success or failure of living during changing times within a changing world.

In nearly every instance, change offers the chance for a better life
Change can be unnerving and unsettling, damaging and destabilizing. It can shorten an organization's life span or redirect the trajectory of one's future. It can be the transformational event of one's life, but far too often, the consequences of change are couched in negative and destructive tones, which is unfortunate because most change has been beneficial to humanity. From medical advances to the liberation of millions in tyranny, from telephones that connect families to technologies that protect communities, change has benefitted far more than has been harmed.

It is change that has advanced the interests of millions over the past generation. Changing cultures, changing philosophies, and changing ideologies have created a society less burdened with segregation, less tolerant of denigration, and more accepting of lifestyle choices. Freedom has become the rule rather than the exception, with inhabitants having greater autonomy to choose their own direction in life and realize their own fate, not one that has been preselected or predisposed.

It has become a different world, an even better world. Martin Luther King Jr. endured decades of discrimination before leading a nonviolent protest for civil rights and in the process changing the way we view others. Ronald Reagan and Margaret Thatcher fought against the confines of communism, liberating hundreds of millions from its destructive practices. Pope John Paul II forgave the man who nearly assassinated

9

him, reinforcing the importance of forgiveness within a compassionate society. Nelson Mandela was imprisoned for twenty-seven years as a result of his fight against apartheid and emerged from prison a man of integrity and grace in the face of humiliating circumstances.

Not all who change our world are famous or seek fame as their reward. There are those who tutor schoolchildren, deliver meals to the elderly, support the Wounded Warrior Project (an organization dedicated to helping those military veterans who were severely injured during their service), and aid the National Autism Association (a parent-run group that provides support to those who have autism). We are indeed fortunate to live among those who believe more in giving than receiving.

These individuals changed the world, creating a better world for themselves and others. They made a difference, and they mattered. They could change the world because they passionately followed the most important rules for enacting revolutionary change: to have the right idea at the right time and for the right reason and to have the determination to make it come true. More than any other theory, practice, or principle associated with change, it is the concept of an idea and the determination to follow that idea to fruition that are the determining factors in the success or failure of change.

Martin Luther King Jr., Ronald Reagan, Margaret Thatcher, Pope John Paul II, and Nelson Mandela are shining testaments that through the power of dreams and the presence of determination, we can create a better life, one person can make a difference, and the world can be changed.

> Change favors those who can adapt
> to the inevitability of a different future.

CHAPTER 2

Reasons to Change

Change can be exhilarating yet destabilizing, transformational yet revolutionary. The consequences of change are evident to many, yet the need for change remains a mystery for some. Why must the very basis of society be shaken? Why must organizations evolve, and why must friends move throughout the world? If change is a natural part of life, a greater understanding of the causes, needs, and impetus for change is appropriate.

There are myriad reasons change occurs, but, in general, the impetus for change can be classified into four, broad categories. They are that something does not work, something could work better, something does not exist but should, and something different.

Something does not work

The first reason to change is quite intuitive: something does not work. It is the least controversial cause of change. If your body does not respond properly to the medicine prescribed by your physician, a different medication is not only expected but also demanded. The pharmaceutical industry spends billions of dollars annually in research and development to devise new medicines to combat old diseases. These medicines impact our lives more than any other change, yet prescriptions to the new wonder drug are scarcely fought.

When the bathroom faucet no longer works, more often than not, it gets replaced by a better version of the same faucet. When automobile tires lose their traction, new tires that displace road water and offer a safer ride take their place. When the computer laptop is dropped and the screen cracks, it is often replaced by a tablet, both because of its ease of use and cost. As products no longer work, either through age or technological obsolesce (try finding a VCR or eight-track player), they must be replaced. They are not often replaced with the exact same products, but rather new and improved versions that offer greater value to the customer.

With the advent of global competition, consumers have greater access to products. Back in the day, you were limited to one or two retail stores to purchase an alarm clock or state map. Now, those products can be purchased online from far away countries, often at a fraction of the price if purchased nearby. Of course, scarcely any people buy alarm clocks or maps anymore as these products have been replaced by smartphones, which have also taken the place of watches and cameras.

When something does not work, consumers are presented with an array of options and alternatives that may not have existed when the product was originally purchased, raising the excitement of today's consumers to buy something better today than they had yesterday. It has become the age of the consumer as new products are increasingly making many old products dated or even irrelevant.

Something could work better
Similar to something that may not work, considerable money and effort are invested in research and development to produce and market products that work better than what currently exists. Opportunities arise or are created for those who can create products or services that are just a little better than what exists, whether they're your product or your competitor's.

The product you manufacture today may make the product you manufactured yesterday obsolete. Apple understood this strange phenomenon, combining the function of its iPod into its iPhone, causing iPod sales to plummet (sales of the once dominant iPod are a fraction of what they were when initially introduced). More recently, the Coca-Cola Company introduced Coke Zero to compete against Diet Coke, and in response, Pepsi introduced Pepsi Max to compete against Diet Pepsi. Both Coke Zero and Pepsi Max are aimed at that segment of the population that may not want a drink with the word *diet* in it, but nonetheless want a reduced-calorie drink.

There is a market for a nondiet diet drink, one with lower calories yet without the stigma some feel with drinking a diet drink. It is true that these new products will reduce the sales of Diet Coke and Diet Pepsi, but Diet Coke is hoping to retain not only Diet Coke buyers but also attract Diet Pepsi buyers; Diet Pepsi has a similar strategy. Coke and Pepsi saw an opportunity to change their diet soft drink product bases and took the opportunity to do so. Change, in this case, was initiated to meet a market need and capture a greater market share.

Tide is one of my perennial favorites. A year seldom passes that we don't see a commercial promoting a new or improved Tide. Whether it is making clothes cleaner, whites whiter, or combining the detergent with fabric softener, Tide always seems to be getting better. In reality, it may not be that Tide is a better laundry detergent. Instead, it is that Tide trumpets one or two aspects of its detergent that may appeal to its customers, while also reminding its customer base that Tide will continually improve its product to meet the needs of the diverse and demanding marketplace. It appears that Proctor and Gamble executives (who produce Tide) believe a new-and-improved Tide will, at the very least, continually remind its customers of the virtue of Tide.

The drug industry follows the same strategy. The industry spends tens of billions each year to research and develop new and innovative drugs. Each dollar spent is intended to create a new drug, one better than the previous one. The United States spends more than any other country in the research and development of drugs and other medical research. In fact, when rulers of some of the traditional and resistant-to-change cultures become ill, many come to the United States for access to the latest medical procedures and most potent medicines. Change is always welcome when it can save or prolong your life.

One other example is interesting to consider. Decades ago, power windows in automobiles were an option; today, virtually every vehicle has power windows. The same can be said for automatic transmissions and car alarms. Of course, new cars also have an array of safety equipment. Some who resist change have certainly hailed these advancements, as they have made driving a car more comfortable and safer, lowering injury and death rates that result from automobile accidents and collisions.

Today, if you do not aggressively and proactively protect your market share—even if it affects the sales of your current product—another competitor may offer that product or service and render your product obsolete. Therefore, organizations must take the opportunity to introduce new products that will compete against existing products, with the hopes of maintaining and even expanding the current customer base before some other competitor does.

Sadly, some companies do not have this foresight. Kodak was the preeminent photography company for over a century but failed to foresee the advent of the digital photograph or smartphones. VHS manufacturers did not heed the rush to DVDs, and many of the companies that once manufactured VHS tapes have ceded their market share to those that manufacture DVDs, though the future of DVDs is less than certain as smartphones and video-on-demand begin to dominate the market.

The same can be said for the average American. The skills and abilities you possess today may not guarantee you the financial and societal security you seek. Innovative products and services come from innovative organizations and their employees, and unless employees continually upgrade their skills, they may be unable to upgrade the skills of their organization's products and services. Like Diet Coke and Tide, a continuous assessment of your skills and abilities and an expansion of your capabilities are vital to succeeding in a shifting marketplace.

The lesson of today may be that the competitive edge—the length of time your product or service can dominate a market—is becoming increasingly short. Unless you innovate and revolutionize your product, service, or even yourself to make it better—even at the expense of your station in life—your ability to control your future will be compromised.

Something does not exist
This may be the most far-reaching cause of change, exhilarating many to the possibilities of something different yet disrupting the

established order that exists. It may be the most fundamentally feared change, as it may create and destroy entire industries. Henry Ford created an automobile industry yet decimated the train industry. Steve Wozniak and Steve Jobs created (in part) a personal computer industry that decimated the typewriter industry. Talking motion pictures largely made the silent motion picture irrelevant, e-mail has decimated the postal service, and the ATM has taken over many of the functions previously performed by bank tellers.

There have been many technological breakthroughs and revolutionary products that have changed and shaped the world. According to some, the most significant product ever created was the wheel (though, going back centuries, some claim the discovery of fire was the greatest innovation as it allowed citizens to heat their homes and cook their food). Directly or indirectly, the design and consequence of the wheel have aided civilizations for centuries.

The wheel allowed citizens to travel and create power. It created a mechanism to trap food, in addition to aiding in food preparation. In fact, nearly every transportation innovation has resulted from the invention of the wheel. Trade and commerce were advanced based on the wheel, either through the movement of goods to the market or the transportation of goods from bazaar to bazaar that eventually disseminated goods to all corners of the earth. It was a seminal event in our history.

Similarly, the discovery of plastic eventually allowed for the creation of satellites and revolutionized airplanes, electricity provided light to the world, and pesticides expanded the production of agricultural crops and helped feed the world. Isaac Newton discovered gravity, Charles Darwin discovered evolution, Albert Einstein discovered relativity, and the invention of the abacus by the Chinese eventually led to the production of the computer. Over the past century, some of the most significant discoveries revolved around medicine. Antibiotics such as penicillin healed the world, pasteurization led to food safety and sterile medical procedures, and vaccines for smallpox and polio have saved millions of lives.

Each discovery—whether through technology or medicine—spawned another breakthrough, often without intention. People are by nature creative and ingenious, constantly searching to do something easier and better. If something does not exist, it could exist with the right mind and muscle to develop and create it, but not without a consequence, and the consequence may not be wholly positive.

Thousands lost their jobs as train travel morphed into automobile travel, online travel bookings replaced the neighborhood travel agent, computers replaced typewriters, and television supplanted radio. While the inventions of yesteryear did displace many employees, those employees who upgraded their knowledge and skills could take advantage of other industries that were created. For every Blockbuster and Hollywood Video that closed, another Jamba Juice or Starbucks opened.

It seems the creative destruction that results in the closure of certain stores and retail chains does not seem to correspond to a subsequent employment increase in other industries. Best Buy electronics stores recently announced a wave of store closings, mainly because more sales are being achieved through its online counterpart or through other online shopping sites such as Amazon.com. Online shopping eliminates the requirement for storefronts (saving expenses related to rent, electricity, and taxes) and sales and clerical employees (customer service is provided via telephone rather than in each store, and checkout can be accomplished without the assistance of a representative).

Historically, science and technology have been at the forefront of creating new industries. Whether in the movement of people (horses, trains, automobiles, and airplanes), medicine (prescription drugs, laser surgery), or telecommunications (telephones, cellular phones, and e-mail), scarcely any industry lasts decades. Instead, innovation propels the conception of many industries, the expansion of some, and the decimation of others. New industries need employees to produce the products and services for the marketplace.

Google, Oracle, and Facebook are relatively new companies that employ a total of more than one hundred thousand employees. Certain industries and companies still recruit new employees, but they appear to be more the exception than the rule. Moreover, those jobs created seem to be traveling overseas as organizations search for lower production and manufacturing costs. Science and technology do not seem to create jobs at the same level of past innovations and product breakthroughs. This circumstance has contributed to the protests by some against advanced countries and multinational organizations.

Today, progress may result in better and more economical products and services, but not necessarily higher employment.

Innovations in science and technology are not limited to the consequences of breakthrough experiments. At times, advances in science and technology stoke the personal excitement and happiness of the ordinary. There is a famous family story involving my son, Gunner, which helps illustrate this situation. Gunner came to the hospital shortly after my daughter, Toria, was born. His gift to her, which he laid in her basinet, was three Hot Wheel cars in a sandwich baggie. He stayed for about a half hour, and then, as we were preparing to leave, he promptly removed those cars from her basinet so he could take them home.

Nothing, it seems, could separate cars from Gunner, including the birth of his sister.

Gunner has been confounded and astounded by automobiles since he was two years old. Throughout his life, he has read hundreds of books and magazines on cars, in addition to traveling to dozens of car shows. He received a new car when he obtained his driver's license, but shortly thereafter bought a beater car that he could rebuild. He now spends his spare time rebuilding and rehabilitating the beater car, adding new devices such as airbags and shoulder seatbelts to make it safer. The science and technology of automobiles has consumed the life of my son, as it has in other areas for many others.

Technology has modernized the cars, concurrently creating a new industry in the restoration of automobiles. In some ways, science and technology may be the least controversial causes of change as medical innovations and discoveries have freed generations from the worry of plagues and epidemics. Science and technology have advanced the health and welfare of generations, but also the jobs and happiness of young adults like my son, Gunner. We also know that change is doing something different, that change is tolerated and even accepted when it advances the interests of those affected, and that those who best adapt to change tend to profit most from its consequences.

In other ways, though, science and technology are the most controversial causes of change. Over the past twenty years, advances in science and technology have not advanced the employment prospects for a wide segment of the middle and lower classes, prompting many to rebel.

Something different
The quest to be different—whether in the manner in which someone thinks, acts, or dresses—has become a fundamental right of today's society. This contradicts centuries of culture that required citizens to respect and adhere to a social contract in relation to language and behavior. In fact, productive societies were often defined by the level of cohesion throughout its ranks, though such customs stifled individual thought and action.

Today, there appears to be more effort to be different than similar. The same pants may be worn high or low on the waist. Pant cuffs may be rolled up or hung on the ground. Even names are rarely similar, even when they are pronounced the same. Mary may be spelled Mari, Merri, or Meri. The differences may be subtle, but they infer that most citizens seek to be unique. Change is more welcome than unwelcome.

Change seeks to do something unique, something novel, something different. It is about making something better with the hope and promise that, at some point, it can make a person better. It will make life just a little brighter and better, whether that be through science or technology. The light bulb created more light than the candle, while the electric car not only offered greater fuel efficiency but also reduced carbon emissions.

Science and technology have the ability to transform the way in which the earth's society lives, but there is an interesting paradox as we search to build something different through science and technology. The scientific and technological innovations that advance our standard of living similarly undermine the stability of an orderly society. We live in a time where dissimilarity is more admired than similarity and where being unique is more treasured than being common. Time progresses, and the world evolves to the consternation of those unwilling to appreciate its newfound and fascinating differences.

Change rarely affects one person or industry, but instead has far-reaching implications on the way in which we live. The bad often accompanies the good. Advances in medicine may prolong the quantity (or length) of one's life, but not necessarily the quality. Some may not want to continue a life of pain or discomfort. Changing technology may create a more powerful cellular phone, but one now manufactured overseas rather than in Ohio or Alabama. Who will have an advantage and who will have a disadvantage is not often known at the inception of change, nor can the long-term consequences of change be determined with a great deal of confidence.

The question is not whether change will occur, for it surely will. Rather, the question is the timing, impact, and consequence of change once it does occur. The quest to think, be, act, and behave differently from your grandparents, parents, siblings, cousins, schoolmates, friends, supervisors, subordinates, coworkers, and neighbors ensures that the world will look different today from how it did yesterday. The great mystery we associate with change is how this change will affect the world in which we live tomorrow.

Time progresses and the world evolves
to the consternation of those
unwilling to appreciate its newfound
and fascinating differences.

CHAPTER 3
The Conditions for Change

Change typically occurs because of the four reasons outlined in the previous chapter. Change can come suddenly or gradually; it can be destructive or constructive; and it can be welcomed or resisted. In most instances, change follows a certain course or path, a path that is affected by certain variables that facilitate change and certain variables that impede change. In essence, change can be more predictable than unpredictable and more controlled than uncontrolled, but the process throughout can be more varied than standard.

It is an art to understand the conditions required to enact and sustain change, and a greater understanding of these conditions enables individuals and organizations to better confront and overcome the financial and emotional challenges of change. An interesting analogy that illustrates these conditions is a ship sailing through the often treacherous waters of the earth's seas, where there are numerous variables affecting the safe and productive travels of the ship. The most important variables would include weather conditions, such as wind, rain, and fog. Ships and boats must also assess the human cost of their staff and the technical challenges of navigating into unknown and unfamiliar territories.

Through wise planning and courage, ships can reach their destination, and passengers, as well as those waiting for the cargo, can reap the rewards of the journey regardless of the change that must be confronted and overcome.

Using the example of a ship sailing through the vast and unpredictable seas, change requires that certain conditions and variables at the very least be researched and assessed. These conditions and variables include:

- The ship must be able to sail.
- The stars must be aligned.
- The galley must be stocked.
- The captain must know how to sail a ship.
- The ship must leave the dock.
- You must know where to sail the ship.
- The captain must steer the ship.
- There must be an emergency raft.

The ship must be able to sail

Success is rarely achieved when change appears unachievable, despair pervades the culture, and failure is a near certainty. The presence of hope, no matter how minute, inspires individuals and organizations to devote their time, effort, and considerable skills to change their present and alter their destiny. Without the presence of hope, change rarely has an opportunity to occur.

Individuals must have the physical ability to change their present situation. A tennis player working to perfect her serve must be able to develop the strength to hit the ball at a high rate of speed. In today's aggressive style of tennis, players without a certain strength and height are at a distinct disadvantage, a circumstance that is nearly impossible to overcome no matter the time, talent, or effort you expend.

US Open champion, Wimbledon champion, and Olympic gold medalist Andy Murray is a great example. His physical conditioning is near legendary as he devotes hours every day to practicing tennis, as well as running and weight training to perfect his body. A well-conditioned body allows him to prevent injury during the physical stresses of a professional tennis match and develop the capabilities to exert strenuous effort over a four-or five-hour period. Talent alone is not the reason that he has become a champion; he has also conditioned his body to withstand the brutal demands of his chosen profession.

The adage that hope springs eternal may offer courage to some, but that courage must be tempered by the reality that success is achievable only through the right situations, conditions, and backgrounds. One must determine the right direction, possess the right talent, and inevitably realize some luck and good fortune. Without that hope, though, change is rarely initiated and the journey seldom continued, especially as adversity and criticism become an expected yet unwelcome variable in the path.

Individuals must have the physical and mental abilities to change their path in life. Organizations must have the financial or human resource capabilities to attain a different future. Ships, too, must have the ability to move, to float, and to sail through any weather and through a myriad of conditions. Without these most basic abilities and conditions met, no amount of time or effort will result in a different future from what exists today.

Once those basic abilities and conditions are met, change is influenced and impacted on the possibility of success, at the very least by the perception that success can be achieved. To tolerate the intense physical work in the gym, Andy Murray must believe it can make him a better tennis player. He must have wins, even small wins, along the way to sustain his efforts.

The future may appear dire, but at the very least, the ship must put itself in a position to succeed. Similarly, a sinking ship must offer its passengers the hope that through hard work and dedication that the ship can be rebuilt, that the rugged journey can be continued, and that the destination can be reached.

The stars must be aligned
Timing is a critical element of nearly any change. An organization must recognize the need for change, or it will cease to exist. Employees must tolerate change or confront the possible end of their career. Individuals must know that without change, their ambitions will remain a distant dream rather than reality. Change initiated at the wrong time confronts a populace opposed to something different, often passionately so because they may not believe danger is looming and an immediate response is vital.

Businesses file for bankruptcy, automobiles will not start, roadways are closed for repair, employees are laid off, and couples divorce. All are forced to alter their paths. The event or circumstance has occurred, and now they can only respond. However, there are so many events that occur throughout our lives whose rise could have been predicated. The totality of the event may not have been predicted, but that the event would occur could have been.

The nation's debt crisis offers an example. As of 2013, the United States owes its creditors almost $18 trillion, not including deficits in the Social Security, Medicare, and other underfunded benefit programs, in addition to untold billions more in deteriorated infrastructure needs. However, for decades now, the government has failed to address this escalating crisis, believing one administration can create the debt that succeeding administrations will have to pay.

With each passing year, the federal debt crisis becomes exponentially worse. It is a tragedy, but the public has not demanded that the government change its conduct (mainly because the public enjoys the benefits produced through the escalating debt), and the stars are therefore not aligned to change conditions that would result in a falling deficit and reduction in debt.

Organizations and individuals who closely monitor their present and future not only can prepare for the eventuality, but also better control the timing and response to that inevitability. Successful and happy individuals realize that a modification in their attitude or character today can forestall great personal tragedy tomorrow. Entering counseling during a strained period of a marriage may prevent its demise, while others may attend church on a regular basis to ensure their minds and spirits are aligned with the values espoused by a certain religion. These actions may save a marriage, strengthen a friendship, change a perspective, or modify one's beliefs and subsequent behavior.

The need to change is inevitable; the only unknown is when. Avoiding or denying the need for change rarely results in a more advantageous future and nearly always results in a more unpredictable or destructive future. It will almost certainly reduce the anxiety or stress that results from forced change before one is emotionally, financially, or physically prepared.

Here is a regrettable example: Most have seen the same effects of totalitarian regimes led by brutal dictators more interested in their political survival than the health and welfare of their country and its people. Somalia and Afghanistan are but two examples, and history is littered with despots who cause the death of millions in their own quest for power and dominance. Too many are unable or unwilling to recognize the ominous signals that foretell catastrophic ends. With more foresight and less denial, some of these consequences could have been avoided or at least minimized and mitigated.

The right time to make a change can often be influenced by a determined leader or a courageous person. At times, the stars may not appear to align, but it falls to the courageous few to change their alignment.

Though the organization may be stable at one point in time, successful leaders convince their followers that the future is uncertain and disadvantageous for the organization on its current path. They passionately articulate the reasons and rationale for a change at this point in time. They raise the awareness of their stakeholders to a more ominous future, one that is certain to occur unless decisions are made and actions are taken to forestall its inevitability. Creating this sense of urgency and rearranging the stars in a different manner reduces your followers' resistance to change since they better understand the need for a different direction and future.

The trick is to choose the right time to make a change, which means you must constantly survey your environment to be aware of the often contradictory conditions that impact your life. One's emotional capabilities may be strong, but their physical abilities may be weak. A strong individual financial portfolio may not be balanced against a weakening global financial system. Rarely does a person get the best cards to play in life, but you must play the cards you are dealt. This means you must choose your own path and be aware of the right time to begin that journey. Otherwise, the failure to choose the right path at the right time has sunk many a ship upon the open seas.

The galley must be stocked
Sailing the high seas requires an exorbitant amount of resources, beginning with a significant number of knowledgeable and competent staff to command the boat. Financial resources to pay the

staff and purchase supplies, in additional to the original purchase of the boat, are a necessity. Emotional and societal resources such as friendship, teamwork, and happiness facilitate the movement from one situation to another and from one place to another.

Drive, ambition, and desire provide the motivation to change; financial, economic, and societal resources provide the ability to change. Someone in an abusive marriage requires the emotional resources to sever the ties of marriage, as well as the financial resources to seek another home and manage a household on a single income. Change is increasingly more complex without the resources to effectuate it. This is one reason change must be planned and methodical. You may know where to go, but you also need to know how to get there and have the tools and materials to carry you there.

Resources are the oil in an engine and wind in our sails. Organizations may want to change the culture of their organization, but may not have the knowledge to do so; individuals may want to change their employment but not have the skills to obtain a better job; and some may want to change a friendship but not have developed the personality to attract better friends.

Assess your advantages and disadvantages, as well as your powers and limitations. Not all resources are within your ability, and those resources should be acquired. Even the strongest companies realize their own limitations and adjust accordingly. Facebook realized it needed a better photo-sharing feature in its social media domain. Rather than develop its own system, it purchased the popular Instagram organization in a deal valued at $1 billion in cash and stock. All have deficiencies, but the innovative adjust accordingly and either develop their resources or acquire the resources from other means.

Dreams may be a worthwhile beginning, but are worthless unless you acquire the means to attain that dream and fulfill its promise. The right resources, both in terms of usefulness and abundance, are indispensable when achieving this dream.

The captain must know how to sail a ship

The captain must know how to sail the ship, and leaders must have the skills and abilities to lead their organization. These skills and abilities differ somewhat depending on the nature of the industry and the aspiration of the adventurer. In general, however, there are four common characteristics that represent people who excel in where to go and how to get there. They are:

1. Talent. They have a talent for what they do (not necessarily general talent). Effort and drive are important, but in many occupations, some natural talent is a necessity. Athletes need physical abilities that come with birth (height, dexterity); a preeminent physician needs certain mental abilities (intelligence); authors need a flair for the dramatic word or phrase; and politicians need some inherent communication skills (voice, height).

2. Work ethic. Talent alone is insufficient. There are many tall individuals who do not have the abilities of Michael Jordan, and there are many individuals with incredible IQs who fail to develop and master their gift. Those who achieve their ambitions have, in tandem with talent, a tremendous work ethic that far outstrips their competitors for greatness.

3. Good fortune. No matter the talent and work ethic, encountering good fortune can be a welcome circumstance. Good fortune and luck are advantageous only if you are in a position to take advantage of it. In 1990, President George Herbert Walker Bush had a 91 percent approval rating. If the elections had been held that year, he likely would have won re-election. The elections were held in 1992, though, and by then the economy had slipped. Bill Clinton won the Democratic nomination for president and presented himself as a compassionate, engaged politician concerned about the plight of the average American. He had the good fortune to run for president during a challenging time for

the incumbent president, but he also presented himself in the right manner to the American public.

Here is another fortunate political circumstance, this time for the incumbent president. In 2004, the economy was stressed, and there was growing opposition to an unpopular war, yet Senator John Kerry lost the election to the incumbent president, George W. Bush. Senator Kerry claims that he lost the election in part because the United States had never changed commanders in chief during a war. True or not, timing may not have been in John Kerry's favor in 2004.

Finally, there are some athletes who reach success because their principle competitor stumbled or the better team had a bad day. In 1990, Stefan Edberg had to default from the Australian Open finals because of an abdominal injury, handing the Grand Slam title to Ivan Lendl. Stefan Edberg may have defaulted the match, but Ivan Lendl still won six matches to make the final and put himself in a position to take advantage of the situation.

Good fortune, yes, but you must also place yourself in a position to take advantage of whatever luck may come your way.

4. The mastery of fear. Without a doubt, those at the top of their profession and field have learned to control and master their fear. Some of this may be genetic or hereditary, meaning a supreme sense of confidence permeates their actions. Mastery of fear includes self-confidence, a belief in your abilities, and a near total aversion to being liked or popular. Those who master fear know their path is often treacherous, but the journey is worthwhile and there is nothing to fear (either physically or mentally), including the criticism and adversity that will most likely be directed toward them along their path.

In my opinion, these four items are either genetic or learned at a very young age. This is not to say that those who do not have those attributes cannot learn how to sail a ship or determine the direction of an organization. Some may have two or three of the above and can learn to be quite good. I would simply offer that it would be more difficult and, more importantly, more unnatural for them to be in a leadership role given the absence of one or two of the above attributes.

The captain may establish the direction, but without working knowledge of how to sail the boat, sailors are dependent on others to attain their dreams. Abdicating your responsibility and creating dependency on others is a terrible way for a captain to steer a boat to the far reaches of the world and attain greatness along the way.

The ship must leave the dock
You may have the greatest yacht in the dock, but you may never experience its speed or magnificence on the waters unless it leaves the dock. This requires courage to move a vessel from the safety of its berth to the risk of the seas. The most detailed plan and articulate speech is for naught without the courage to move from concept to reality and to at least try to reach for the stars.

Change means something different; something different often requires the movement from where you are to where you should be. Knowing where to move or what to change to is important; summoning the courage to make that move may be the most challenging aspect of change for management. The right direction is a necessity. Without the right direction, you may be wandering aimlessly throughout your life without ever reaching your destination. Too many spend their lives dreaming their dream without ever developing the confidence or fortitude in achieving their ambition. It is a shame.

Very little changes unless you move from one idea to another, from one strategy to another, and from one hope to another. Change requires the movement from security to insecurity, from the known to the unknown. It is a terrifying journey, but one that might offer a better future than the one that exists today, and we move forward with the realization that what exists today is unlikely to lead to a rising or better standard of living. Choices need to be made, and challenges must be confronted and overcome.

For anything to happen in life, you must *do something.*

Thus, the path of change begins with the ability to move followed by the willingness to move. At some point in your life, you must do something that will ultimately define your life's existence. Your ship must leave the safety and security of its surroundings if you are to explore the natural wonders of the world. You must *do* something in order to *be* something, which is often why too many feel powerless to change the circumstances of their lives.

You must know where to sail the ship
A ship may sail through the seas, but without a direction, it is a rarity that the ship will reach its destination. In truth, a ship will always reach a destination, though not necessarily the intended destination. Prolonging the destination through circuitous routes may also heighten the risk and danger involved and cause additional expense and unnecessary time. For these reasons, most entrepreneurs create a detailed business plan, and most ship captains follow a precise map.

Plans and maps are important for several reasons. First, they indicate you have studiously analyzed your past. You understand all facets of the journey, including how one aspect affects another and which aspects of the enterprise require more attention than others. A competent and detailed plan means you have analyzed the mistakes of the past, ensured present strategies reflect the avoidance of these mistakes, and highlighted future hazards.

Within organizations, plans provide clarity to the shifting societal, political, and economic variables of your industry, whether that be the global economy, industry threats, new competitors, customers, or suppliers. All of these have to be assessed to understand and determine the capabilities of your organization. Only then can discussions regarding your future have clarity and merit. The second rationale is to utilize plans and maps, because maps provide the direction of the organization. They raise awareness to the complexities that lie ahead, and this knowledge allows the captain to alter the intended direction toward a safer path. In particular, plans indicate you have consciously thought about your goals and how to achieve them. For those who lead or manage an organization, plans are forward-focused, meaning that they detail the actions to consider to reach a future, but also reflective of past hurdles and mistakes. By analyzing problems and situations that may affect the future sustainability of the organization, the plan appears more reasoned.

Rare is the plan that is perfect upon its inception;

common is the plan that can be improved upon its implementation. Competent plans and maps showcase the studious inquiry and thoughtful pursuit of your intended ambition. That realization can raise the awareness and respect for the direction forward.

Most obviously, plans and maps state your path, direction, and destination. This map is useful not only for the captain and owner/leader, but also investors and employees. They provide an opportunity for others to review your direction and destination and offer critical advice and suggestions that may improve upon your plan. Those involved in the endeavor can identify, debate, and debunk challenges to the plan, including benchmarks and critical issues, and offer appropriate alternatives. Rare is the plan that is perfect upon its inception; common is the plan that can be improved upon.

In the best of circumstances, ships demand maps to sail the nautical complexities and far reaches of the seas, organizations demand maps to venture through a complex global marketplace, and individuals demand maps to journey through an unstable economic and societal environment. In the worst of circumstances, the absence of maps produces rudderless entities unable to determine their direction or control their destiny. They become victims of circumstances, which, at one time or another, were within their control.

The captain must steer the ship

Every country has a chosen ruler, every organization has an appointed figurehead, and every ship has an anointed captain. Not every ruler rules, though, nor every captain commands. That said, any change of substantial effect—including those who direct and create the future—requires a person who has the will and fortitude to make the right decision at the right time and for the right reason.

Ships do sail, and they will eventually reach a destination, even if that destination is at the bottom of the ocean. It is the strong nature of a unique person who determines the direction and then fights the inevitable battle among those involved whose position may be negatively impacted by the destination. The battle at Barnes and Noble, the nation's largest bookseller, offers an interesting example of steering a ship in a direction not welcome by all involved or impacted.

Barnes and Noble, along with other book retailers, has moved aggressively toward eBook and other online book-reading ventures. Hundreds of millions have been invested in this enterprise, often at the consternation of those who work in the brick-and-mortar Barnes and Noble stores. Vast resources are being diverted to this online venture rather than expanding stores, providing promotional opportunities, and raising the salaries of employees. It is an interesting paradox: The neighborhood Barnes and Noble storefronts generate the funds to move toward eBook and online sales; if successful, the neighborhood Barnes and Noble storefront that provided that opportunity would pay the price in terms of closed stores and unemployed workers.

Like the leaders of Barnes and Noble, it is the courageous captain who steers the ship into choppy waters, but the destination can never be reached in any other manner. Progress creates winners and losers, even when the losers realize progress is in the long-term benefit of the organization. This is why change is so difficult and so rare. Success comes and goes, and it is the chosen few who sustain success over the long term. Since the level of resistance to change is in direct proportion to the level of loss that some will confront, change is often dependent on those individuals willing to make the sacrifice and pay the price to enact and sustain change.

Now more than ever, change requires a person who is impervious to criticism and adversity and follows what is right regardless of any professional or personal repercussions. The world needs such strong and vigilant captains who take hold of the wheel and guide the rudder into the calculated and intended direction that benefits the whole rather than the few, the future rather than the past. Regrettably, not many such captains exist, which is one reason our world faces such a perilous future.

There must be an emergency raft
Change means going from the comfortable to the uncomfortable, from the safe to the unsafe. As a result, there is risk and some uncertainty as to whether the change may work. Is the change too passive, too aggressive, too incremental, or too fast? It may be the right plan but the wrong time. Likewise, it may be the right time but implemented in the wrong organization.

A host of variables affect the success of a plan, some of which may be predicated and controlled, some of which cannot be adequately accounted for. For that reason, ships must have an emergency raft, and organizations must have a contingency.

Since the future cannot be predicted with certainty, the plan is often modified or adjusted as it progresses. Even if you have developed the perfect plan, you cannot accurately determine how your employees will act or how your competitors will respond. The ability to anticipate the reaction of the human being is an art rather than a science, which is why fights and wars rarely end as predicted.

The back-up plan assumes that the means are expected to be adjusted to reach the ends. The economy, weather, competitors, customers, finances, attitudes, emotions, and employees all conspire to complicate ambitions. No amount of research and thought can eliminate its affect, though it can be minimized.

Boats carry emergency rafts because the journey cannot be predicated with certainty. Organizations develop contingency plans because customers and competitors vary with the wind. Each is sought to raise the level of confidence one has about the future and to raise the feeling of security that leads to a more balanced, steadier life. Each is a pivotal component of a competent change management strategy.

When is the right time for change? Under what conditions can change be enacted and sustained? These are questions that vex even the most forward-thinking organizations and individuals. The best laid plans can be complicated by their design and implementation during an emotionally draining or financially strained time, no matter their importance to the future.

As mentioned, change is rarely welcome or accepted unless there is a clear and distinct benefit to those impacted. That said, change does not always impact individuals equally or similarly, and there are winners and losers in nearly any change. The stars are not always aligned to encourage change, but organizations and individuals can conduct research and attempt to mitigate the various conditions that affect and facilitate change. You must have the basic ability and capability to change, the timing must be right, the resources to sustain change must be plentiful, you must have the courage to make a change, you must know what direction to go, there must be a strong leader or manager to make that change, you must know how to get there, and you must always consider an alternate plan if the original one falters.

Change may be inevitable, but failure is not. Understanding the conditions under which change is initiated and the factors that affect change as it progresses are variables that can affect whether your path ends at your intended destination or your unintended destruction.

Dreams may be a worthwhile
but are worthless unless you achieve them.

CHAPTER 4
The Definitive Change Process

As outlined earlier, the clever sailor begins with a map. Likewise, the gifted musician begins with sheet music, the adept builder begins with blueprints, the gifted writer begins with an outline, and the accomplished cook begins with a recipe. Physicians conduct medical procedures, actors follow a method, managers implement strategic plans, and scientists conduct experiments. All begin their process with a road map as success is rarely achieved by happenstance, coincidence, or boredom.

Road maps, processes, and procedures dominate our world. Those initiating or implementing change should also follow a prescribed format to raise the possibilities of success. Some steps are intuitive and are to be expected. Other steps, however, are unique because of the human factor or motivational element that greatly influences the outcome of the change process. As an example, the start of the change process depends on expansive research to determine the proper direction, but that direction is often reached through the efforts of those impacted by the change. The human factor, then, should be of paramount importance in the change process.

Change should begin with exhaustive research and end with dramatic inspiration. Generally, the definitive, comprehensive, and methodical change process would follow these eight steps:

- Step 1: Research the past, present, and future.
- Step 2: Describe the perils of complacency.
- Step 3: Describe the thrill of adventure.
- Step 4: State where we must go.
- Step 5: State how we will get there.
- Step 6: State when we will get there.
- Step 7: Identify the critical factors that may impact the process.
- Step 8: Inspire others to achieve greatness.

Step 1: Research the past, present, and future
Each component of the change process is important, but research plays a critical role for a number of reasons, including:

- It establishes the background and foundation upon which the intended change is determined.

- If you have continually investigated and researched your industry, market, organization, the global economy, the political climate, and societal factors, you have critical knowledge that can help you prepare for a different and potentially difficult future.

- If you have continually researched your environment, during periods of trial and stress, you will have assimilated the information necessary to make an informed, yet rapid, decision. This action saves time and anxiety that often results from periods of stress.

- Too many decisions and actions are determined without the proper research to support the course of action. In these cases, an individual or organization is relying solely on their experiences. Without a broad and comprehensive background, one's experiences are not sufficient enough to rely upon to make consequential decisions.

Research should be at the forefront of any decision that is made. Success is difficult to achieve without devoting the time and effort to identify the possibilities. After years of traveling the country, my friend John Ellis believes there is an outstanding opportunity to create a consulting firm to provide advice to struggling restaurants. He has developed a keen eye for what works and does not work and feels there is a market for his advice. Surely, he would not have identified this opportunity without the considerable research associated with his past travels.

Those creating a firm need to perform the research and analysis to determine whether a market exists for their product and whether they have a competitive advantage against others in the market. Those leading and managing an organization must continually research the market to determine the viability of their enterprise and how to reenergize their operations. Research provides the information to make a knowledgeable decision. Decisions without research have a greater degree of risk and uncertainty, both of which do not inspire confidence in others as you move to change the direction of your organization.

Step 2: Describe the perils of complacency

Few generations have experienced the rapid and continuously changing landscape that confronts today's generation. In these turbulent times, it is understandable that so many search for stability, security, and a semblance of serenity. However, the marketplace does not respect and reward serenity, especially as the world's consumers demand the latest version of the iPhone, latest flavor from the ice cream store, and the latest style of blue jeans.

Timing is an interesting factor in the change-management process. It is an art to determine the right time to change, mainly because the greater the risk associated with change the greater the apprehension to embark upon it. For those individuals and organizations enjoying prosperity, the impetus to change may not be pronounced as some ponder why rocking the boat is necessary. But scarcely any can state with any high degree of certainty how long the success of today will last.

Unsettling economic, political, and societal times; an acceptable present situation; and concern about an uncertain future can solidify the need for complacency. Choosing what is of greater comfort than what can be, especially if there is a chance that what can be may be less beneficial than what is. In any event, unhinging the death grip that people often have on sameness and complacency can test even the most skillful leader and manager, but it is a necessity worth pursuing.

Complacency leads to sameness, and sameness leads to obsolesce. Scarcely any products that existed in 1910 exist today; in fact, few products that existed in 1970 exist today, at least in their current form. This fact is not driven by the organization, but rather the consumers who want something better for their retail investment. This fact raises an interesting paradox: Consumers demand something different from the marketplace, and that is acceptable, yet employers demand something different from their employees (better customer service skills, broader technical capabilities, etc.), and that is often deemed unacceptable. And therein lies the lesson of complacency: Whether an entrepreneur or employee, those who cannot or will not innovate are doomed to be insolvent and unemployed.

Research is a principle tool in overcoming complacency. Through exhaustive research, the perils of the past and their impact on the future can be brought to the attention of others. It is still difficult to discount solid conclusions based on impartial data and information, even though more rely on emotion to determine their future than reasoning and logic. In any event, efforts must be devoted to crafting a credible case as to why the continuation of the present imperils the ambitions of the future.

Step 3: Describe the thrill of adventure
What is a true shame is how the fear of failure—at times, a consequence of tremendous risk—prevents some from experiencing the rush of exuberance and the thrill of adventure. It is a rarity for success to be achieved by riding the same horse year after year. Sadly, at some point the horse ages or tires, and another horse is needed. The same is true of an idea or a product; at some point, a new idea or product is needed to reinvigorate a person or organization.

My children are fascinated with the height, speed, and daring twists and turns of roller coasters. We have experienced all the top roller coasters in the United States, including Dollywood in Tennessee and Cedar Point in Ohio. Nothing can compare to those first couple of seconds, strapped and harnessed into the safety seat, just before the roller coaster goes from zero to sixty in about three seconds. I yell, my daughter screams, and at the end of the ride, my son asks if we can go again. Some may think that thrill of adventure is hard to replicate, but it can be done by persons of boundless energy and passion for a different, yet better, future.

There are not many events that create more anticipation, more enthusiasm, and more apprehension than trying something that has never been done or does not have a higher degree of success but, if successful, will result in a tremendous windfall. Such is the nature of adventure that creates a sense of excitement incumbent on embarking on a thrilling journey to unknown ends.

Once the perils of complacency have been expounded upon, a person or organization must quickly pivot to address the fear that may result once people realize sameness is no longer tolerable. They are searching for the next journey, and their apprehension should be addressed in a rapid manner so that anxiety does not turn into stress, negativity, and resistance. The aperture to transition from complacency to adventure is narrow, but is vital to address.

If the emotion related to complacency for the present can be traded for the excitement for the adventure of the future, tension will be redirected toward working for a different future. Rather than fretting about the past, that anxiety will instead provide the fuel to reach the goals and ambitions for a different future, one that holds greater promise and the opportunity for a sense of safety and security that we seek in a changing world. This is where the thrill of adventure can overtake the perils of pessimism that seem so prevalent throughout organizations today.

Step 4: State where we must go
Surrendering the security of the present for the uncertainties of the future can cause anxiety and stress. A key responsibility of a change agent or leader is to clearly detail the goal or destination of the change. That future should be interesting and exciting, to be sure, but better than what now exists. Finally, unless that future is perceived as attainable, the endeavor is hopeless.

Confusion reigns when the future is unclear or ambiguous. The statement that "our future lies with the North," could mean North Dakota, North Carolina, or simply north of your present location. Efforts are squandered to determine the destination, wasting precious time and diverting attention from the true ambitions. At a time when change shakes the fragile psyche of those involved, confusion further erodes people's confidence.

By their very nature, most people are not creative, confident risk takers. This is one reason many work for someone else rather than pursuing self-employment; in the United States, only about 10 percent of the population is self-employed. The ability to depend on someone else offers greater comfort than depending on oneself. Interestingly, that belief offers less security to the average person because you have abdicated your own future to someone else, and your survival is now dependent on others rather than yourself. In theory and in practice, this is a terrible situation to inhabit.

Embarking on an unknown future requires faith and courage. It also requires considerable knowledge about the challenges and opportunities that may lie ahead, and then work to take advantage of that future. You truly create a different future. Identifying and communicating the future you hope to attain is central to ensuring that those within the organization or your sphere of influence will direct their energies toward that worthy goal. It will alleviate the anxiety and stress that can pervade a changing circumstance and offer greater confidence to others than the future is known, the path is evident, and attainment of this new reality will be in the best interests of all included in the adventure.

Step 5: State how we will get there
Adventures in foreign lands can be exhilarating. The sense of excitement can be overwhelming to some. Foreign lands bring new experiences, but also the challenge of adapting to a new way of life, including a different language, lifestyle, customer, and culture. All can be daunting, especially for those unaccustomed to unusual and dissimilar experiences.

It is interesting that expectations of anxiety when traveling and visiting foreign lands to places unknown and unusual is planned and anticipated, yet similar changes within an organization related to a new position or compensation structure are not. In both scenarios, resistance of change is diminished and acceptance of change is enhanced when those involved not only know where they are going but also clearly understand how to get there.

Some seek the excitement of an unplanned and unscheduled life, believing that not knowing what comes after every step can enhance the sense of wonderment seen in so many children. There is much truth to that belief, but not in every circumstance. Change that is forced can be detestable to even the most ardent adventurer, a circumstance that can be addressed by creating a detailed map highlighting the method and manner that will ultimately lead to our destination. Moreover, the map highlights the time and thought invested in a different future, providing those who follow an opportunity to provide constructive advice and input on a more effective path to follow.

A comprehensive, well-thought out plan or map raises the confidence of those impacted by the change that the venture is not one of folly or coincidence. Instead, it portrays an approach that can be debated, criticized, revised, improved, enhanced, and modified. Such a map can address the anxiety inherent in traveling in foreign lands or embarking on a risky business venture, while raising the level of involvement and commitment from those most impacted.

On one side of the change coin is knowing where you need to go; the other side is knowing how to get there. If you know where you need to go but not how to get there, your time and money will be wasted. If you do not know where you need to go, but can go everywhere, you will end up somewhere but not necessarily where you need to be. In nearly any circumstance, success favors those with a laudable goal and a competent plan to achieve it.

Step 6: State when you will get there

Comprehensive and useful plans nearly always include the who, what, and why aspects of the issue at hand. Inevitably, the when becomes a common refrain, as well. The when becomes especially important when change involves sacrifice—for example, how long will we have to sacrifice before we receive our rewards, or, in some cases, how long do we have to put up with this before we know if it works?

For projects of great magnitude and in times of great instability, time may be the principle challenge or opportunity. Many will sacrifice for a short duration if the reward is sufficient; few will sacrifice for a long duration if the reward is insufficient. Thus, reward and time are intricately woven. Teams and coalitions will also be sustained in the short term during challenging times, but tend to fray and even disband over longer periods of time. This is why the term *strike hard and fast* has relevance when embarking on the unknown and treacherous.

As the time involved lengthens, the ability to achieve small gains or wins is crucial. These wins can hold together a fragile team and embolden an often unwilling coalition to withstand and overcome conflicting personalities, emotions, and interests. Wins show that the road is right, the journey is worthwhile, and the plan has been well conceived and implemented.

On the other hand, defeats of any magnitude can cast doubt not only on the plan but also the ambition. Bickering and dissention can then disrupt the cohesion needed during these challenging times, distracting attention that should be focused on overcoming hurdles and impediments. These hurdles and impediments oftentimes do not arise until the plan has been implemented and its flaws and mistakes become known.

Time can be a great advantage and disadvantage. The presence of time allows a plan to be designed, implemented, and modified as it progresses. The absence of time challenges even the best laid plans as pressure is more prevalent to achieve the ends in an expedited manner. In any case, the time involved with any change plan or process should be honestly determined and disseminated to all those involved and impacted. This not only answers the when question but also raises the level of confidence that those involved may have in the plan to achieve the change. However, this confidence will be sustained only if the time frame is realistic and attainable.

Step 7: Identify critical factors that may impact the process

There are a multitude of issues that determine the success or failure of a change event. Some events benefit from the right vision, appropriate financial resources, and a motivated staff. Other events are challenged by management inertia, lack of staff competence, a highly competitive marketplace, and changing social mores. These factors affect the success or failure of a change venture, and these critical factors must first be identified and then be mitigated to not affect the outcome of the process.

At the commencement of the project overview or strategic plan, consideration is given to seminal events, often discussed in the timeline portion. For example, does the organization have sufficient financial resources? What is the likely response by industry competitors to this organization's change in strategy? How will labor unions respond to the change in the employee compensation formula? All are critical factors to the success of a plan. While answers to these questions may not be conclusively resolved during the planning stage, they must be identified and debated, and a competent plan of action must be determined prior to the implementation of the plan.

Rarely, though, does a plan go as envisioned. While some critical factors may be identified prior to the change process, others may not be clear until the plans implementation. Or, in an increasingly likely scenario, the assumptions underlying your strategy may have been inaccurate and misguided. Therefore, continued vigilance is essential to identifying and mitigating critical factors as the plan progresses.

Critical factors may raise the cost of the plan, delay the implementation of a strategy, or preclude an organization from realizing the benefits or rewards from the intended change. Some of these factors can be mitigated before the plan is implemented, some can be mitigated if and when they arise during the process, and other factors may not become apparent until the plan is implemented. In any case, there must be a concerted and coordinated effort by the plan promoters to determine factors that may arise and impact the process, communicate these factors to affected personnel, and determine a prudent course of action should that factor arise.

Step 8: Inspire others to achieve greatness
Before nearly any sporting event, coaches step before their players and galvanize them to achieve greatness. They state that the game can be won, that it should be won, and that it must be won. They remind the team of the practices they have attended, the sacrifices they have made, and that all is in preparation for this game at this time.

Reminders and philosophies can be inspiring messages for others. There are two I have utilized extensively during contentious and calamitous situations. Both inspire me to make a difference and hopefully inspire others on their quest for greatness. They are:

- You should always look for the good along the road of life. Never search for what is wrong, but for what can be made right.

- Go down swinging: The fear of failure and the fear of what others think have destroyed the ambitions of most men.

Never underestimate the impact of motivation and inspiration on the ability and will of an individual or team. Through hard work, risk, dedication, and courage, you must believe that the goal can be achieved. Without this belief, doubt and a lack of self-confidence will constrain your ambitions, allowing your mind and body to betray you at the most inopportune times. You become tentative in your thoughts and hesitant in your actions, which inhibits the faith and courage most needed as you undertake your quest.

A reminder that you have invested greatly in your venture, that you are physically and mentally capable of achieving your dream, and that you simply cannot be deterred or defeated can be an inspiring call to action to begin the change. It is why generals talk to their troops before battle, managers talk to their employees before organizational restructurings, and presidents talk to nations in times of peril and crisis. It reassures and ignites the passion and drive needed to overcome the impediments and challenges in an uncertain future. This call to action may be the difference between apprehension or anticipation, doubt or surety, and success or failure.

Whether it is a car, house, or job, not many circumstances last in this life. Cars must be replaced, houses rehabilitated; once-stable organizations crumble. Change is frequently a destabilizing event for people in every walk of life. Change can be moving from a home, becoming unexpected parents of twins, or losing a friend.

Change is a certainty, and those most prepared for change are those most able to profit from it. More often than not, change fails because the process to facilitate the acceptance and implementation of the change was either not developed or not followed. Without such processes, you raise the level of apprehension, insecurity, anxiety, and doubt, all of which may impact future success. The hope is that you identify the process most conducive to your circumstance and then adhere to its tenets while remaining flexible as the environment responds to your chosen direction.

Thankfully, there are a number of theories and processes created to better understand change. Most processes include a considerable focus on research, direction, communication, and inspiration: research the history and the future of the circumstance, identify the direction to embark upon, communicate thoroughly among your stakeholders, and inspire those involved that the goal is realistic and the future is attainable.

Change is a process that requires concentration and deliberation. Identifying the appropriate processes to follow provides focus and a sense of stability during changing times, and also raises the confidence level that those involved have in the chosen future. Processes reignite inaction, reinforce action toward a predetermined goal, ensure that projects remain on focus, and bring stability to those in an uncertain world.

Go down swinging . . .

The fear of failure and the fear of what others think have destroyed the ambitions of most men.

CHAPTER 5
The Change Agent

Leaders have certain skills and abilities. Great leaders are passionate about their chosen pursuits, charismatic within their circles of influence, and possess unparalleled character. They may have other characteristics, but those three skills and abilities are most representative of a leader.

Successful managers, too, have a certain set of skills and abilities. Successful managers like what they do, are knowledgeable about their profession and industry, work hard, have superior organizational abilities, make work fun, and are good and decent people. There are exceptions, of course, but successful managers have a high degree of these skills and abilities no matter the country or industry they work in.

Without question, the ability to propose, promote, and manage change requires a definitive set of skills and abilities. Some of these skills may be common to a leader or manager, but a change agent is focused on a specific duty or task, often for a finite period of time. This is one reason there are rarely change agents employed by an organization. Instead, there are more often consultants engaged to perform their task in a specific situation and an expedited time frame.

The skills and abilities unique to effective change agents and the desire to acquire and master these skills and abilities can make the difference between success and failure for those in the change management profession. These change agent skills and abilities include:

- Having a natural curiosity of the world
- Being impervious to failure
- Being impervious to criticism
- Being driven yet patient
- Being able to make tough decisions
- Being a likable person

Natural curiosity of the world
The history of change is littered with one word: different. It is about thinking different, acting different, and being different. Change is creating a unique product or modifying a novel service. This requires a different type of person, one who rebels against tradition

rather than bowing to it and one who challenges the future rather than accepting the future as something that cannot be altered.

Few phrases encourage a different thought or approach better than "what if." What if we use a different ingredient in our chocolate chip cookie dough? What if we swim farther into the ocean to explore the natural habitat of a particular fish? What if we discontinue our most profitable product and instead invest our research and development monies on a new product with a potentially spectacular windfall?

What if we institute an innovative loyalty program that rewards current customers rather than enticing new customers into the store? These what-if statements allow you to question the reality of today and ponder the possibility of tomorrow, and they all have the desire to see if something different can work in common.

In nearly any situation, people are eager to think that problems can be solved, issues can be resolved, and challenges can be overcome simply by questioning the circumstances of the day and believing that those circumstances can be changed.

There are those who seek order and logic in the known world, believing that there is a smooth path to be followed that evades stress and anxiety. There are others who seek wonder and excitement in the unknown world, a world meant to be discovered and conquered. They believe there are deeper waters to explore and taller mountains to climb and that innovations and inventions represent the pursuit of a worthwhile life, one that satisfies their hunger for adventure while raising the hopes of the populace.

These individuals have a natural curiosity of the world, and whether that curiosity involves the search for renewable energy or regenerating cells, the world is rewarded through the pursuits of these ambitious and utterly unique individuals. A common attribute of explorers and inventors is this natural curiosity, bolstered by an unquestioned belief that what has been imagined can be created and that what has been imagined can be reimagined. They have an unparalleled and unrivaled wonderment in the possibilities of the future and a hunger to at least try to make things happen. Challenges and setbacks are to be expected, even anticipated, but should not interfere or impede our curiosity.

We are a world dependent on these rare, curious individuals who believe that problems can be solved if something different can be done. It is through this natural curiosity that our energy needs will be resolved, diseases will be eradicated, hunger will be diminished, and hate will be banished. The quest for greatness begins with curiosity.

Impervious to failure

The fear of failure has destroyed the ambitions of most people. They believe failure will become the imprint of their life and that it will define who they are and what they are trying to do.

I have met many individuals who have achieved great success yet have never experienced great heartbreak. Great accomplishments and great rewards often come from great sacrifice. Part of that sacrifice is surely time and money, but also the sacrifice of pride and respect that is the inevitable consequence of ambitious men and women.

Change replaces the security of what is known for the insecurity of what is unknown. Strategies and practices that may have been successful in the past may not be successful now, and modifications and adjustments must be made to ensure the continued success of the organization. Had McDonald's Big Mac been sufficient for fast-food dominance, the Quarter Pounder and Happy Meal would never have been developed. Success breeds complacency, which fosters laziness, with failure becoming the all-too-common consequence.

Those who work to arrest complacency are often swimming against the tide of acceptance. Organizations and their members are enamored with the present and are fearful of the future. Many believe that anything different or that change of any kind will result in failure and strive to convince all involved that stability rests with maintaining the status quo. Those who oppose the status quo are believed to have a rendezvous with failure.

The fear of failure can cripple even the most confident. The broader the repercussions of failure, the greater the trepidation and anxiety involved in changing course. This is why being impervious to failure is a critical attribute of those who want a different direction and of those who work to change the future. The ability to tolerate and even welcome failure is exceedingly uncommon. While assuming the risk of grand ambitions is to be lauded, few can tolerate the repercussions of failure, which is why substantive change is a rarity that is to be admired.

The great advances in history arose through failure. Failure is the precursor of success, a development achieved only by those impervious to failure.

Impervious to criticism
Those whose life work revolves around the critical pursuit serve very little purpose in the lives of their fellow citizens. Their desire to crush the hopes and destroy the dreams of others is a contemptible trait, one that undermines the very fabric of friends and foe alike. A question often asked is why people place such value in the thoughts and minds of others.

There is an inherent fear of criticism and of not living up to someone else's expectations. In the eyes of the criticized, others will mock and make fun of their ideas, goals, and ambitions. It is a complex, yet fascinating, phenomenon—that our sense of value does not rest in our own minds and bodies, but in the impressions and opinions of others.

Whether these impressions are valid or unsound or credible or fallacious is not in debate. Especially at a younger age or maturity, whether these opinions are true is dwarfed by the need to be liked and admired. For too many, what seems to matter is the impressions and opinions others hold of them. The awareness that others believe we are stupid, cowardly, or worthless casts a debilitating spell on our self-image and self-esteem, which paralyzes even the most determined and confident. The desire to take chances, strike out on your own, and strive for something more, as well as the need to do something different, all become forgotten ambitions as far too many become debilitated by the derogatory or degrading opinions that others hold of a life they do not lead.

Such is the power that others can have on your life if you let them.

Most perplexing is that we surrender our sense of self-worth when we listen to the degrading and demanding opinions of others. I have long believed that there are two types of people in this world—those who applaud efforts and those who applaud failures—and that you should always look for the former. Those who applaud failures are consumed by hate, jealously, and envy. They seldom criticize to make you better, but rather to deflate the life you lead in the hopes that it will inflate their own.

In reality, it is not your self-worth they are trying to impact, but rather the negative and worthless image they have of their own life. It is a sad commentary of a failed life, one that is destined to be void of value or admiration. It is the life that they have chosen to live, but that does not need to be the life that you choose. Therefore, those are not the opinions and impressions that should impact you.

Conversely, those who applaud efforts believe that success is achieved through efforts rather than results and that you are judged by the desire to try rather than by whether you win or lose. This is the type of people we should have in our life; this is the type of people who deserve our attention and respect.

It is unfortunate, even sad, that some people's self-worth is determined not through their own beliefs but through the jealous, envious, and hateful opinions of others. It is a terrible way to live. Life will be destined to be devoid of joy and happiness when lived in this manner. But it is not the life that you need to lead. Being impervious to criticism may be uncommon to the many, but it is common to the few, and it is those few who truly change the world.

Driven yet patient

Drive and patience are nearly perfect complements. Drive promotes ambition and determination, while patience promotes acceptance and tranquility. Can one strive to accomplish tasks within a given time frame yet be lenient when stated goals are not achieved? Can one be driven to succeed yet tolerant of setbacks and failures? Though these traits may not easily coexist in a single person, for those consumed with the exhilarating task of initiating and sustaining change, this coexistence is an absolute necessity.

Drive is fundamental to growth and progress. My father and mother are incredibly driven individuals. That drive has resulted in success beyond their imaginations, yet they continue working. I have inherited that trait, working considerable hours in public service and then running a successful writing and lecturing business. The drive to sacrifice and work hard is central to changing and advancing one's station in life, a lesson long learned from my parents.

Patience is an agreeable trait for the lazy; it is a disagreeable trait for the driven. Change rarely follows a straight line, so too much drive must be restrained during inopportune moments. It is these adjustments and modifications in thought and action that can enable continued progress.

Dreams are ethereal concepts that encapsulate our hopes for the future. Without the drive to achieve them, dreams remain dreams. The reality is that dreams are achieved through hard work, perseverance, and dedication; change is achieved by the desire and drive to realize the future you believe is possible. Those espousing change in their marriage, organization, and life have a belief that it can be better, but it is the strength and endurance of their drive that will determine whether their hopes can become reality.

Uncontrollable drive may lead to success in certain situations, but can often will lead to a ruthless, selfish, and disrespectful environment, one that will promote an ever-increasing divisive atmosphere. This is a principle reason that an unfettered drive must be tempered with patience—the ability to recognize that variables affect even the best-laid plans, and reasonableness and accommodation can coexist with drive. It may not matter when you get to your destination as long as you reach your destination. Such delays may not be catastrophic and can allow additional time to rethink the destination of your plans, along with the process designed to achieve them.

Driven individuals are those who see something different and have the desire to change it. Patient individuals realize that the world cannot be changed in a single instance or day. Driven yet patient individuals are at the heart of change. They have the desire to achieve something different, yet realize that extraordinary achievements are rarely achieved without setbacks and heartbreaks. Emblematic of a driven yet patient individual is one who has the ability to dream mightily yet persevere over obstacles. It is the rare individual who encapsulates both attributes, which is one reason change is so elusive.

Make tough decisions

At times, making a tough yet unpopular decision can prevent a crisis or at least lessen its severity and impact. At other times, when the tough decision is not made, or not made at the right time, the situation can spiral out of control, causing untold damage and dissention among those involved. Even worse, the inability to make the tough decision only delays the inevitable. The decisions that must be made later may be more draconian in nature because of the escalated crisis.

Why were the necessary decisions and actions not made earlier? The answer can often be quite simple: The decision was difficult to make. The necessities to fire some employees, reduce the pay for other employees, or move production to lower-cost states or countries are gloomy choices to consider. The impact and implications of those decisions are wide-ranging and gut-wrenching, leading some to delay or defray these decisions in the hopes that the situation will recede and that the need to make these decisions will fade as conditions change.

Decisions are not unique to a person or situation. Throughout life, we must determine which course to take and which path to follow. Should we attend a public or a private school? Should we purchase a house or continue to rent an apartment? Should we remain at our current employer or seek another one? Should we eat at McDonald's or Taco Bell? Not all situations are complex, and not all decisions are significant. That is gratifying, but decisions must nonetheless be made that affect the direction of your life.

That said, decisions are also not, technically speaking, difficult to make. You assess the situation, determine possible causes and solutions, and select a solution that is most favorable to resolving the situation. It sounds easy enough, yet the greater the impact of the decision, the greater the difficultly in making the decision. To many, the impact of divorce is greater than the impact of marriage. Socially and financially, the impact of a divorce can be calamitous. The impact of maintaining your current employment versus resigning and starting your own business is less menacing to most. For many, the uncertainty of self-employment is too great a risk versus the security of a steady paycheck. Of course, that is one reason those who are self-employed or business owners typically earn a greater income—they are willing to assume the risk.

Decisions are easy when the risk is minimal and the reward is great. Not many delay the decision to make more money or eat more chocolate. But as the consequences of a decision become more perilous, few stand ready to take a chance. The ability to make the tough, unpopular decision that is in the long-term best interests of those involved is an uncommon attribute. It is, however, a common trait to those willing to risk an unstable present for a stable future. It is an essential attribute for those willing to confront a grim situation, take a tough stance, and make a difficult decision. Your stance and decision may not be successful, but it at least gives you chance to make something better. In this volatile world, few take this chance, but it is those who do who create the world others will live in.

Likable personality

A person who seeks to change the world is destined, at some time and in some way, to confront an antagonistic public determined to thwart even the most noble of intentions. They enjoy the present or at least fear the possibility of a more disadvantageous future. Resistance can turn toward hostility and outright rebellion at the slightest hint of the possibility of failure, reinforcing the belief that actions were misguided and ambitions naïve and improbable.

People are accustomed to the life they lead, enjoying the habits of talking with the same friends, living in the same neighborhoods, and working in the same industries. There is an element of sameness that is attractive. People are drawn to others who believe and live in the same manner, so those who think and act differently are fated for a somewhat solitary and lonely existence. It can be discouraging, but it can also be inspiring.

Those whose motives are decent and noble, believe in the righteousness of their cause, and pursue their ambitions no matter the adversity or criticism encountered may indeed encounter negativity. But they also garner admiration and appreciation. People respect those who take a stand, maybe because they do not have the courage to do so themselves or believe that these people will stand up for them if and when the occasion ever arises. They like such people, and the ability to be liked is of great value when you embark upon creating something different.

A kind word, a thoughtful gesture, and even a smile are representative of a genuine and caring person, one more interested in the advancement of others than his or her own advancement. It is a person who does so with a clear mind and a pure heart, though he or she may pursue contentious ambitions. Detractors may arise, but their arguments lose some relevance as the unselfish aims of those seeking constructive change are mirrored against the selfish aims of those resisting positive change.

Likability is the perfect attribute of those seeking to do something different. It is the perfect shield to disarm critics and the perfect banner to attract supporters. Finally, it is the perfect representation of how people should treat others and the inner peace and happiness that comes to those who choose to be that type of person.

It takes little ingenuity or creativity to manage operations consistent with well-established guidelines, practices, policies, and procedures. You need only continue on the road that has been planned, rarely deviating from the map that serves as the guiding light. In most cases, you will arrive at your destination, on time and on budget. However, given the ever-evolving nature of today's marketplace, is the destination in your original plans the destination that should be your ultimate plan? It is an interesting question to ponder.

Decades ago, the competitive advantage or edge of an organization could be exploited for many years. The long-term investment in a new venture that required a long-term marketplace dominance to recoup that investment was not uncommon. Today, however, an organization's competitive advantage does not last long, reinforcing the need for an organization to maximize their benefits, and to continually evolve as an organization. This is why a natural curiosity of the world, impervious to failure, impervious to criticism, to be driven yet patient, to make tough decisions, and to be a likeable person are important attributes and are becoming more representative of those who aspire to change their station in life than those static skills and abilities so common in earlier generations.

The quest for greatness begins with curiosity.

CHAPTER 6

The Realms of Change

Each realm of change has its own unique challenges and complexities. Some seek to change the world, while others strive to change their family. Organizations believe their products will change the way you live; politicians believe their policies will change your standard of living. Boyfriends and girlfriends are convinced that, once married, they can change their would-be spouse, while job applicants are convinced they are the missing link needed for the employer to return to profitability.

But can you really change the world? And for that matter, can you really change someone else? Are you the only person you can change? Finally, are the skills, abilities, and motivations needed to change the world the same as those needed to change your family? These are certainly questions to ponder as you explore the vast complexities of change.

The outcomes of change are often similar. You create something different tomorrow from what existed today. But the process you follow to create that difference will surely vary depending on your ambitions, and that should be understandable. The same skills needed to change a country may not be the same as those necessary to change a culture. The techniques needed to lead a technology firm are different from those needed to run a political campaign. Similarly, the emotional stability to be a good spouse would be different from that needed to be a good employee. Different situations require different abilities, and different abilities require different approaches.

There are some commonalities, of course, and many of these commonalities have been discussed whenever and wherever the subject of change is discussed. However, circumstances and complexities exist that should be considered and debated based on the intended focus and desired outcome of your change ambitions. Rarely is one size fits all a realistic approach, and the same can be stated for change.

Recognizing the subtle and overt differences in each realm of change may be the difference between triumph and tragedy. These realms and their particular complexities and opportunities are:

- Change the world
- Change a country

- Change a culture
- Change an organization
- Change an employee
- Change yourself

Change the world
Changing the world seems to be the ambition of the very young and the very old. The young, especially those of college age, believe that unfairness can be overcome and injustice can be ended. They believe that equality should permeate throughout society and that people have the ability to determine their fate unimpeded by the influence of others. Their youthful exuberance is admirable, though it can be misdirected and misplaced at times.

The end of discrimination and equal treatment under the law are beyond debate. However, not every difference throughout the world is an injustice. Those with the interesting idea, the tolerance of risk, and the willingness to work hard often achieve a higher income than others. It is not an injustice but a consequence of sacrifice and ambition. Some countries squander their natural and economic resources and then become dependent on the grace and favor of their fellow countries for survival. This is not an injustice but rather a consequence of a lack of political and societal will to live within their means.

The very old strive to change the world as they become closer to their destiny and assess their legacy. They want to be known for something other than the status they achieved and the money they banked. They realize that those attributes do not represent a life of substance—only a life of material. For that reason, they reconsider their accomplishments and the impact of those accomplishments. Some become disappointed with their efforts and disillusioned with what they did with what they had. They question their worth and search for the value that can be achieved only in what they leave behind for others and in how they have changed the conditions of advancement so that others can achieve the hopes and dreams that will define their own existence.

Andrew Carnegie may be one of the best known contributors to the greater good. Toward the end of his life, he donated much of his fortune for the construction of educational institutions and libraries. In fact, his money built more than 2,500 libraries, including the one in the town in which I now work.

Others have been just as generous. Bill Gates and Warren Buffet are donating billions for the pursuit of eradicating diseases and educating the youth. John D. Rockefeller and Marshall Field founded the University of Chicago, which Mr. Rockefeller claimed was his best investment. Walt Disney helped fund the California Institute of the Arts, Henry Ford created the Ford Foundation to distribute his billions toward charitable works, and Howards Hughes gave his billions to establish the Howard Hughes Medical Institute. All had one commonality: They did so toward the end of their lives, after realizing a lifetime of wealth accumulation did not satisfy their need for meaning.

Money may come and go, and for most it goes, but institutions and buildings tend to last for generations, with the names attached to their buildings a permanent reminder of a life lived in service of others and contributions to mankind.

Age changes the perspectives of man. People think deeply and broadly as the end comes. The realization of what people have accomplished prompts them to use what they accumulated toward temples of magnificence. Whether those temples include eradicating guinea worm disease (by former President Jimmy Carter) or founding Vanderbilt University (by railroad baron Commodore Vanderbilt), these accomplishments are often seen as the singular mark of their time on earth.

What personal traits and characteristics does it take to change the world? Some of these traits and characteristics, of course, are similar to those of a change agent. But there are other traits and characteristics unique to those who aspire to great change and great significance. These traits and characteristics would include:

- Authority. Change of any scale or significance requires the authority to determine the direction and the means to get there. Some may possess abundant skills (which is the ability to make change), but without the authority to utilize those skills, the scale and scope will be limited.

Recently, Rad Bartlam, the city manager of Lodi, California, requested that I restructure and re-engineer one of the city departments. He and the board of trustees in charge of leading the department granted me the necessary authority to initiate structural and systemic changes throughout the department. The message to staff was clear: The very nature of the department would change, without delay and without exception.

Seven months later, the department had a new mission statement along with specific ambitions to be achieved within a finite period of time. Service standards have risen while the number of employees has fallen; working hours have increased and overtime has decreased; and customer visits have grown and customer complaints have dropped. The department has been refocused and reborn, providing far better and more expansive services to the community, realizing greater value for the financial contributions from the city, and enhancing the long-term job security for those employees that remain.

It has been a remarkable achievement, proving that public services can be improved without a corresponding increase in financial support and that will and tenacity can overcome apathy and inertia. But without the unequivocal support of the city manager and board of trustees, the endeavor could never have left the dock or remained afloat throughout its arduous journey.

Those who change the way others live typically have the right to do so. For good reason, few have that right, and the hope is that those who do use that authority for the good of humanity rather than their own grandiosity.

- Resources. Remaking and redrawing the future on a global scale demands resources of great significance. A candidate for the president of the United States requires considerable more financial resources than a candidate for mayor of a small town. Likewise, global change requires resources on a global scale.

- Ability to communicate. While you may have the authority to force change, power is a helpful tool to convince those outside to your authoritative rights. The ability to convince, cajole, and persuade can be used to great advantage and expand the range of your influence. Martin Luther King Jr. and Rush Limbaugh are two individuals who had no particular authoritative base but used their powerful oratory skills to entice an audience and sway their opinions.

- Crisis. Though not a skill, it is necessary for global change. The presence of a crisis weakens resolve and raises susceptibility to an inspiring (though potentially dangerous) message from nearly any source.

The need to leave something of significance and admiration behind, through the creation of charities and buildings, becomes a driving force as we age. The desire to change the world and create meaning for our lives consumes our minds and bodies toward this noble pursuit, which (sadly) few obtain. It does so in the eternal hope that we will stand for more at the end of our life than we did when we were living it.

Change a country

The United States is a much different country in the twenty-first century from what it was in the twentieth century. For those who believe such change is inevitable over time, there are countries across the globe that appear to be stuck in time. Afghanistan has changed little over the past years, and there are many countries in

Africa that have progressed little—either economically or socially—over the last fifty years.

Three variables appear to largely control the probability and degree of change within a country: age of population, economic system and growth, and strength of religious conviction. As the age of the population skews younger, there is a higher prevalence for opportunities and a rising standard of living. The disenchanted youth want a more promising future, leading to rising societal instability and a more militant demand for change (perhaps any change that is different from the bleak present) consuming the lives of the discouraged youth.

Economic system and growth refers to the country's political system. Controlled political systems such as communism, socialism, and dictatorships suppress independent thought and action, leading to an inherent rebellious nature (though suppressed because of considerable danger) unless economic growth is prominent. Capitalism leads to a stable society as ambition and work are rewarded, unless rewards are distributed unfairly and not in accordance with effort, level of work, and skills and abilities of the individual.

Strength of religious conviction denotes the influence and control religion exerts over a country's citizens. Those countries whose religious beliefs exert a controlling effect on its citizens, as well as the desire to adhere to those religious traditions, can impede change. The countries in the Middle East represent these fervent beliefs. Those countries whose religious convictions are less pervasive may promote a more progressive culture, one less constrained by tradition. The United States is best representative of this school of thought. Thus, the strength of religious conviction can influence a country's propensity to change.

Changing a country is compounded by other factors, including the size of the country (it is more difficult to change Russia than Monaco, for example). Multiple languages and homogeneity also complicate the landscape, as witnessed by the multitude of languages spoken in the United States, whereas Japan has only one, general language spoken by its people. Finally, a country's location on the world map is a factor: Countries in Europe are exposed to a wider range of influences than islands in the Pacific.

A natural curiosity and being impervious to failure are attributes needed to change a country, in addition to the following that are more unique to this type of change:

- A following. Individual initiative may raise the issue, but there also needs to be a groundswell of support to carry that message to the masses. Martin Luther King Jr. had the right message at the right time, but also the organization to broaden its impact. An individual can be patronized and dismissed, but a movement whose time has come is difficult to dismiss. The movement to resolve the nation's immigration situation is another such example, as large protests have propelled the issue to the forefront of political minds.

- Resources. Similar to changing the world, financial and societal resources provide the channel to disseminate the message to a broad spectrum of a country. Ross Perot was able to finance his 1992 presidential run without any prior political experience because he had billions in the bank. The same went for New York Mayor Michael Bloomberg. Resources do not necessarily translate to victory, but they provide a person with the platform that he or she can then exploit to pursue his or her interests.

- Ability to gauge the time and mood. An idea whose time has come means that either the idea was brought by the right person or the right idea was brought at the right time. In either case, you must astutely gauge the mood of the populace to determine its receptivity to a changing future. The right person can create the right time, yet at other times, the right time can create the right message. Timing and patience become more critical factors as the scope of the change increases and its impact broadens.

Change a culture

Culture exists in any environment. Quite simply, it is the way things are done. If you wash your hands before dinner, that is a part of your culture. If you say please and thank you, your culture represents that conduct. If you stand when women walk in the room, that is learned through your culture.

Culture plays an important role in society. It is the framework or set of rules that its members follow in order to be an accepted member of that group. It details the acceptable and inacceptable behaviors in order for someone to inhibit an environment. In essence, it tells people how to live within a certain environment at a certain time and serves as the social glue.

For the most part, culture has a binding or constricting influence. Since culture consists of rules of expected behavior and conduct, these rules are intended to guide your actions to within the confines of the established culture. Some rebel against these confines, especially the young who believe it hinders their freedom of choice and expression. This is a primary reason political unrest typically occurs at times and in areas where there is a high prevalence of young people. Egypt and Syria are countries with a high percentage of their population under twenty-five years of age, and this contributes to the political instability occurring at this time. In the United States, the baby boom after World War II meant the 1960s were a decade of great political unrest, especially at universities and colleges.

Culture can also hinder the creativity of its members. Upon joining a team, you learn the acceptable behaviors and thoughts, whether relayed to you in writing or verbally. Violating these explicit or implicit rules can bring scorn and ostracism to the new person on the team. For that reason, culture that restricts thought and expression can have an intimidating consequence on its members. This is a reason culture can have a destructive force on its environment unless it has a clear purpose that benefits the future of the group or of society.

Questioning the validity of certain rules and conduct within a culture may give rise to a contentious situation, but it may be a situation that should be addressed if the long-term health and viability of that entity is to be assured. It may be determined that this particular aspect of culture is wise and beneficial and should be continued. It may also be determined that the current culture may be restrictive and harmful and may eventually be destructive, possibly causing the eventual extinction of that environment or that group. In these scenarios, raising the issue should not be derided but applauded as it affords the opportunity to assess the way things work, maintain those that do work, and revise those that do not, all of which benefits its members.

Changing a culture requires a number of skills and abilities, with imperviousness to criticism a primary attribute. Not remaining silent in a staff meeting if you are a new employee, when it is expected, or not completing tasks at least two days before the scheduled due date (again, as expected) may be cause for conflict or discipline. However, there may be a valid and constructive reason why those aspects of culture should and must be debated and modified.

Culture, then, should be debated and modified as time progresses. The relevant, appropriate, and beneficial culture of today may be the irrelevant, inappropriate, and harmful culture of tomorrow. Besides an imperviousness to criticism, what type of person is best qualified to change culture? An individual with these additional characteristics may be the best qualified for this endeavor:

- A friendly demeanor and disposition. Changing the way things are done, often after years of consistency, is far less offensive when the change agent possesses an optimistic, respectful, and friendly personality.

- Persuasiveness. Culture does not change a person, but rather a group. Therefore, you need the ability to communicate your opinion to a broad group in a way that changes what it has been taught or, in some cases, the only thing it knows.

- Knowledgeable. Being against something or someone, even passionately and aggressively, is more simplistic than proposing what should replace it. Consequently, those who want to modify a culture should be fully knowledgeable about the culture's history, its advantages and disadvantages, what aspects could be maintained, and what aspects could be modified to foster its effectiveness.

Changing a culture can be a creative transformational event, one that advances the overall interest of the group. Of course, you must change the culture for the betterment of the group, which is the stated reason that change occurs in any environment.

Change an organization

Certain governments (communists) dictate the jobs their citizens do. Some governments (socialists) dictate the pay people receive, which is largely the same across occupations so there is a sense of equality of outcomes (regardless of whether there was equality of effort). Finally, other governments (capitalists) believe you could choose the job that would provide you with the means to live. This is the prevalent ideology in the United States, though the government still exercises considerable influence in the position you choose because of rules, taxes, and regulations (you must have certain certifications or licenses to perform given occupations).

In each of these governmental structures, a great majority of working citizens work for some type of organization. In the United States, only about 10 percent of the population is self-employed, though they may create a business that employs others. Individuals create organizations to produce a service or product for a customer. A structure within that organization is created to facilitate this ambition. These founders, and the leaders and managers they hire to run these organizations, create a system that fosters productivity and profitability. That system is maintained through a labyrinth of policies and procedures to ensure its goals are met. It is a controlled system, one that naturally becomes more static and resistant to change as the years progress.

For every rising Facebook, there is a fading MySpace. Blackberry eventually gave way to the Apple and its iPhone, which is now being challenged by Samsung. Maintaining the continued vibrancy and relevance of an organization—in fact, changing that organization—requires organizations and members who have drive, patience, and the ability to make tough decisions. The following are other, more specific characteristics.

- Organization that tolerates dissent. An established organization is inherently resistant since past success propels an organization to continue on its current trajectory. People might wonder why they should listen to someone who is not responsible for past successes. Without an outright failure, most organizations and their members resist change and those who propose it. Therefore, if the organization does not tolerate dissent, it will continue its journey until it meets its unfortunate collapse.

- Unwavering support from an owner/executive. From large to small organizations, the chance of enacting real and substantive change is directly proportional to the unwavering support of its owner and chief executive officer. Similar to changing the world, you must have some authority to propose and implement decisions in your chosen environment.

Top leaders and managers may be some of the most vocal opponents of change, fearing the resulting loss in status and income that change may bring. In fact, top leaders and managers may be the cause of the current difficulties, and consultants hired to address these difficulties may be thwarted by existing management. Consequently, owners and leaders must be vocal proponents of organizational change and provide change agents with the authority to implement change no matter the repercussions, including the loss of their own status and position.

- Clear link between idea and reward. It is not difficult to change something that does not work to something that does work; it is more difficult to change something that works to something that could work better. To reduce the resistance of those within the organization and gain the tacit support of some members, ideas must be viewed as plausible and possible. Their implementation must be seen as something that may significantly raise the long-term employment prospects and income rewards for its members.

- Be willing to lose your job. Changing something that *is* to something that *could be* requires an act of faith from those affected by the change. Employees may lose their job, their income, and their basic livelihood, all variables that will raise their resistance. Moreover, organizations typically falter because of managerial ineptitude or incompetence. Proposing and implementing changes to your division or department explicitly highlights the mistakes of your managers, a fact that will surely impact your long-term employment at that organization. Sadly, this is a primary reason change agents and creative thinkers do not enjoy long-term job security.

  Proposing bold reforms raises the risk involved in such proposals. The odds of success may be low, but the odds of failure would be high without the effort. Be willing to lose your job fighting for what you believe in, and your passion and perseverance will serve as a model of confidence during strenuous times.

- Intelligence. The perception that you are intelligent instills confidence in your decision making. Flying into the unknown is less daunting when your pilot is unquestionably the best. Few traits are more revered than a brilliant tactician.

- Altruism. The individual with pure motives—a kind, generous, honest, and unselfish soul—earns the respect of colleagues and enemies alike. We are instinctively drawn to decent and honorable people who remind us that right always triumphs over wrong, kindness always triumphs over hatred, and goodness always triumphs over evil.

Organizations are created because individuals cannot produce enough services or products. They grow because they become successful. Changing an organization is a challenge unless the organization has failed, and it may be too late by then. To be sure, consistently reviewing organizational objectives, products, services, employees, and processes is essential to ensuring an organization changes as the world inevitably does. Identifying and supporting those key staff members whose intelligence and ambition are dedicated to making the organization relevant in an increasingly competitive marketplace is likewise essential.

Change an employee
Applicants become employees because they succeed in the recruitment and selection process. Once employed, the employer learns who the employee truly is, while the employee becomes influenced by the culture of which they are now a part. All of this impacts the long-term productivity and happiness of an employee.

Undoubtedly, organizations must hire the right person. It must be a job the employee wants, the organization must continually train an employee to upgrade his or her skills, and there must be specific expectations and repercussions for that employee in that job. To change an employee, he or she must clearly and explicitly know the way in which to change.

In my experience, employees should always meet these four expectations. If not, they should be expected to. They are:

1. Focus on the customer. We have a job because we have a customer, and without a customer, we are without a job. You must ask how each detail will benefit the customer. Every

decision must be decided in the context of providing service to our customer.

2. Do good work. The world is replete with talented people who have done little to perfect and utilize their talent—superb painters who never market their paintings because they fear criticism or phenomenal writers who do not publish their books because they fear failure. That is a shame. Nearly any superstar you meet in life—those who achieve spectacular success and achieve phenomenal ambitions—possess great talent in their field, but then they work hard to perfect that talent. Great accomplishments and great rewards often come with great sacrifice.

3. Do something good. I often ask people what they have done with what they have. It is an interesting question that allows people to talk about the advantages they have and then tell us what they have done with those advantages. Dreams are great, as are ambitions, but at some point, you have to do something with them. In that light, work hard and do your best to make a difference every day that you work.

4. Concentrate on what's next rather than what's past. Your destiny is determined by what you do tomorrow, not yesterday. Never look to the past with regret. Instead, look forward with ambition and hope. Always believe that there will be taller mountains to climb and more fascinating buildings to construct. It will give your life purpose and a sense of genuine excitement and adventure in all you do.

Some employees will not meet these expectations, yet their conduct and behavior may be salvageable. Changing an employee requires the talents of a likable person yet one who makes tough decisions. Moreover, there are other attributes needed by an organization or manager to change an employee's behavior or conduct.

- Noble ambition. Organizations that offer their employees a chance to improve upon the landscape often have a more motivated workforce. Money and power are enticements to some employees, but the pursuit and attainment of noble ambitions has a more far-reaching impact to many.

• Care about your employees. Good organizations care about those who devote their efforts to its success. To me, care is defined as genuine concern for someone else's health and well-being. We endeavor to work for those who care because they have a high sense of honor and duty. We respect their dedication to their employees, customers, and environment. They care to do the right thing for the right reason at the right time. They simply care to make a contribution to others.

• Embrace the differences in each person. Employees remain in groups and organizations where they feel valued and appreciated. These groups and organizations choose to do things a bit differently. They have a different approach, one that is unique in the marketplace to differentiate themselves from their competitors. This is accomplished by eliciting the innovative and intriguing contributions from employees and customers alike, knowing that only through such endeavors can the ideas of tomorrow be generated.

You need to not only tolerate differences but also demand them. It will elevate the spirit of camaraderie throughout your organization, drawing employees into a group with unique thoughts yet shared ambitions, and strategies on how to achieve these ambitions.

There are many influences in a person's life, including family, friends, churches, and neighborhoods. Employees are influenced by their organization, their managers, their coworkers, and their customers. The varieties and complexities of these influences should lead organizations to ensure they maximize the positive contributions of their employees while minimizing those attributes that may negatively impact employee development and organizational productivity. It is the assessment of an employee's abilities, and a constant reassessment of those abilities as an organization and its environment evolves, that leads to the retention of the right employee for the organization.

Change yourself

The most resisted and difficult change is changing your own beliefs, values, attitudes, emotions, and basic disposition. Our world seems to encourage the trajectory of our lives not primarily influenced by our own choices and actions, but rather by the influences and control of others. We appear controlled and manipulated by our employer, coworkers, teachers or schools, businesses and organizations, and the government (any type of government at any level). It is as if we are puppets whose paths are determined by the indiscriminate whim of someone or something outside our control.

It is a hopeful wish to be able to absolve us of the mistaken and misguided consequences of our choices by blaming someone else. But, it contradicts a basic premise of this world. For most people, you do have a choice as to where to live, what to do, what to be, and what to become. The only variable is whether you choose to exercise that right or abdicate your responsibility to follow the life chosen by someone else.

The statements "It is not me" or "I can't believe that this has happened to me" betray the truth that you have become the person your previous actions have created and that you have placed yourself in a position for "that" to happen to you. You become and became a victim because you failed or neglected to take control of your present to create your own future. The fault, which too few realize, lies in the life you have chosen to lead, and the consequences and repercussions of that life have created the happiness or sadness that pervades your very thought and action.

Acknowledging the unfortunate choices of your past and their impact on your present is a key realization to changing the path of your future. The few who do so begin the difficult and often painful journey to rehabilitate and redeem their lives. It can and must be done to achieve some semblance of peace at the end of a life.

It takes a unique person, one who has laudable characteristics, to take responsibility and change one's life. In addition to an imperviousness to criticism and failure, such a person would possess the following additional characteristics:

- The ability to accept responsibilities/blame. Changing yourself requires the understanding and acknowledgment that the responsibility for the general direction of a life, including its successes and mistakes, lies with the person living the life. It is similar to driving a car on the freeway. The manner in which others drive affects the operation of your vehicle, but you are largely in control of where you go and how you get there. Accepting any deviations along that road lie, in most cases, with the person at the wheel.

- Maturity. In our youth, we make decisions based on attracting friends, fighting against the system, and being cool. The need to "go along" appears stronger than "go alone," and we become more susceptible to succumbing to peer pressure. As we mature, we gain the maturity to think for ourselves and choose a future that is more consistent to where we want to be rather than where others want us to be. We separate ourselves from friends and family, and the result is a life more consistent with our own hopes and dreams. Unfortunately, few possess the strength of character to develop this characteristic in our wayward youth.

- Unembarassable. Similar to an imperviousness to criticism and failure, the ability to choose a direction without regard to the judgment of others is a singular characteristic of someone willing to change themselves.

Margaret Thatcher was believed to be completely unembarrassable, a trait that allowed her to choose her own path in life. Tolerating embarrassment, ridicule, and scorn is terribly difficult, but nearly essential to becoming the person you will look back on with peace and pride. Changing yourself is the most difficult change of all, but it is certainly the most rewarding and relieves a person of not only living someone else's life, but also making the most of the life he or she leads.

Construction is often segmented into corporate, commercial, and residential; marketing is often focused into geographic, product, or customer (such as government, corporate, and consumer). One size fits all is not a successful strategy, whether in construction or change, as most have different circumstances and ambitions. The ultimate probability of success is dependent (at least in part) on crafting the right strategy to the right audience at the right time. Doing so can change the world, a country, a culture, an organization, an employee, or yourself.

> What's right always triumphs over what is wrong,
> kindness always triumphs over hatred,
> and goodness always triumphs over evil.

CHAPTER 7
Three Ds and Two Cs

Change is an arduous venture because there are winners and losers. If all were winners, the word *losers* would be relegated to the trash heap of history. Inescapably, the higher the stakes and the greater the rewards, the more contentious the struggle and more convoluted the process.

The process of change is a learned skill. Books and seminars tout the latest strategy on how to enact change, and the strategies in this book are another attempt toward that end. However, change that has the greatest chance of success explains both the how and why of change.

There may be captivating reasons as to why change is proposed and enacted, but unless those reasons are conveyed with a sense of urgency and excitement, the likelihood of widespread support for this change may be fleeting. More than nearly any other variable, that may undermine efforts to transform the present set of circumstances.

How best to convey this sense of urgency and excitement to galvanize support for change? What is the best strategy to answer the important question of why this change is being proposed now, and why it must be implemented today? The message that conveys the answer to these questions should be compelling yet constructive and motivating yet memorable. It must not rouse the mind and the heart, for that which ignites the passion in others offers the energy to overcome timidity and insecurity.

Change can magically transform a person from where they are to where they should be and reshape a future without hope to one without limits. The most constructive and profound change occurs when you have the right dreams at the right time and for the right reasons. This is when you have the determination to make the painful sacrifices and tough decisions emblematic of great people, when you are given the chance to do so, when you are absolutely confident in your direction and outcome, and when you truly believe you can make a difference.

There are endless potentials and possibilities in a life, but only if you so choose to embark on a different future fraught with great risk but also with the chance of great reward. The three Ds and two Cs best represent where to go and how to get there when you take the opportunity to do and be something different.

D Dreams that are right and just
D Determination to make painful sacrifices and tough decisions
C Chance to make that difference
C Confident in the direction and outcome
D Make a difference in some way

Dreams

Dreams matter and have consequences. The right idea can lead to a rebirth of a generation, while the wrong idea can lead to devastating ends. Dreams and their far-reaching implications are the reason that determination is needed. The attainment of those dreams is what makes a difference.

Where do dreams come from? The best dreams come from our passion, that intense desire that consumes our life. The passion to follow our hopes and dreams and to spend our time doing what brings us the greatest sense of pride and satisfaction. It can be eliminating hunger in Africa, tutoring children after school to raise their grades, or donating funds to rebuild a cherished city building. Few have the same passion and dreams, yet it is the pursuit of those unique passions and dreams that can transform our future.

Dreams come from other sources, as well. They come through great research and investigation, in questioning the status quo, in proposing and defending a thought, in listening to the doubters, and in reshaping your dreams as new information becomes available. Dreams are best determined when you ask not "what is" but instead "what could be" and when you consider the eternal dream of something new and different.

Dreams are the powerful beacons to your future. Through dreams, your direction is determined, and if achieved, your fate is realized. It starts with the dream, but does not end with hope. It ends through hard work and resolute determination and in the determination to make others believe both in the idea and your ability to achieve it.

Determination

Regardless of the prevailing idea and the fortunate opportunity, the chance to achieve prominence rests on one elusive variable: the determination to make the tough decision, take a stand, stand up for injustice, and stare down those in the path of an idea whose time has come. Few have the determination to be different, do something different, and sacrifice all with the slim hope that the uncertain future is preferable to a comfortable present.

Having the determination to do what is just and right is not easy. Most are taught to go along and get along, to do that which attracts applause and appreciation, and to respect the established culture of society that restricts conduct and confines ambition. Roadblocks, impediments, ridicule, and ostracism are tools used to ensure compliance and adherence to the way things have been. Predictably, few break the shackles of societal pressure to lead rather than follow and confront rather than conform.

The willingness to defy the odds, stand alone against the masses, invite scorn, and risk failure are attributes of so very few, but it is these very few who the rest of the world follows. The efforts to rebuild our public education system against powerful special interests, the struggle to restructure organizations that results in scores of layoffs yet offers a greater chance for its long-term viability, and the fight to reform Social Security and Medicare so benefits are fair to both current and future retirees are events of such magnitude and consequences that few have the determination to take a chance. For that reason, determination is the singular, common trait that defines the mythical leaders of our history.

Chance

There are those who have the chance thrust upon them and those who create a chance. Elected politicians who excel during a time of a national crisis (Israeli Prime Minister Golda Meir during the Yom Kippur War, British Prime Minister Winston Churchill during World War II, President George W. Bush following the September

11 attacks, and President Abraham Lincoln during the Civil War) often rose to the pantheons of great leaders.

Others simply created a chance. Pope John Paul II advanced the concept of an Eastern Europe free from communism, British Prime Minister Margaret Thatcher devoted her premiership to unburdening the chains of socialism from Great Britain, South African President Nelson Mandela fought for equal rights in his African continent, and Susan B. Anthony and Elizabeth Cady Stanton battled for a woman's right to vote. All believed in a different future, regardless of whether they often stood alone.

Change can be envisioned, researched, planned, and articulated, but it still must be implemented. It could be the right idea at the wrong time; the best person may be hired in the worst organization, one unwilling or unable to support a radical rethinking of its business operations. You may take the chance that presents itself or create the chance against often considerable odds.

In reality, the greater likelihood of success rests with those who have the ability to determine its implementation. Their support is crucial to ensure that those involved in the change process, or impacted by its consequences, do not thwart or sabotage a future they may not support.

An idea whose time has come. The civil rights movement and suffrage encompassed decades of heartbreak, eventually resulting in a shift in the hearts and minds of a nation that no longer believed that one race or sex was inherently better than another. The time came after incomparable struggle and sacrifice, through rising awareness and unrelenting pressure that inequality and injustice is not representative of the human race. The time came after realizing that society is only as decent and good as it treats its fellow citizens.

Passion and fortitude are essential yet lonely virtues when the fight is right but the timing is wrong. At some point, the time comes, the chance presents itself, and the battle is won. Defining change depends on dreams and determination, to be sure, but also a chance given or taken to make that difference. This is one reason change is such an elusive circumstance in a society.

Confidence

Stability is welcome to those interested in preserving the status quo—when a person is satisfied with their employment situation, financial status, or personal relationships. It is the rare person, however, who is fortunate to live a life without pain, sacrifice, and instability. In fact, success and happiness comes not from evading loss and disappointment, but instead from overcoming the losses and disappointments that are the inevitable consequences of leading a daring life.

Every life has a direction; some have the determination to change that direction when the results and outcomes of that direction are less than desired. Most become powerless to change their circumstances. It is a most unfortunate circumstance because only by changing the scenery of your life can you hope to see a brighter sky and witness a more striking sunset.

Change typically results from or causes volatility and instability, at least in the short term. Some people change because their present is crumbling; other people change because their future is worrisome and bleak. Both scenarios foreshadow an era of unpredictability, where doubt and anxiety cause hesitancy and indecision, further paralyzing one's ability to think rationally and act quickly to improve their situation.

Dramatic and revolutionary change is best achieved in a stable and certain environment. Predictability of events and certainty of outcomes may not always be achieved, but they are admirable goals to strive toward. In a time of instability, projecting an aura of confidence strengthens your own fortitude and that of everyone affected by the process and outcome of your endeavor. People want to believe that a different direction will be better and that their future will be brighter. They want to be secure in where they are going, knowledgeable in where they are going, and confident in who will take them there.

Confidence is the utter and complete belief in who you are, what you stand for, and where you are going. It is a certainty of purpose and an unwavering faith that you know and can do better. The way forward may be rocky for many, even perilous for some, but those who possess the sureness in their abilities and confidence in their ambitions will become leaders of men, offering the best hope to change one's circumstances and shine the beacon to a brighter light.

Make a difference
Some are drawn by money, others by fame. Money and fame rarely last, though; the stars of today are often the unknowns of tomorrow. Too many people and things come and go, and this lack of permanence means that those drawn by money and fame will lose their motivation once those variables fade.

Those best suited to excel during changing times are those who believe in what they are doing and where they are going. They believe their work creates something that improves upon the world in which they live. They may be teaching others to read, feeding the hungry, communicating with those who cannot hear, helping the disabled walk, curing the sick, assisting the unemployed to find gainful employment, and holding the hands of those in pain.

They strive to create a better future, one in which they may not benefit but others they have not met may. Their focus is the advancement of others often at the expense of themselves. They become a better person simply because it is the happiness of others that is of paramount concern, not the fame or fortune that may fall before their feet once their good intentions and deeds become known.

It is those who want to make a difference that endure the uncertainties and difficulties associated with great change. Through struggle and challenges, the will to make something better for others overpowers the will to make something better for ourselves. A sense of pride and hope pervades those whose interests far exceed their own, and this ambition can be intoxicating for the individual and others who come to believe in the power of a different, yet better, future. It is this type of person who seeks to make a difference in the lives of others.

In the dawn of life, we strive to make a living; in the twilight of life, we strive to make a difference. As first-time parents, we seek others to raise our children; as first-time grandparents, we seek to raise our grandchildren. In our younger years, we abuse the environment for our own pleasure; in our later years, we work to save the environment for others' pleasure. As young adults, we squander our money on frivolous pursuits; as we age, we save our money for sensible expenses. Education and maturity change our perspective as time advances.

Can you imagine if we strived to make a difference throughout the entirety of our life? What if we worked to save the environment, shelter the homeless, and feed the hungry in our younger years? What if we helped those with speech impediments to speak more fluidly or advised high school seniors on how to weather the life-altering experiences as a college freshman? Quite possibly, we could have changed the trajectory of their future rather than waiting until their fate had been determined.

Too many have spent more than they have saved, used more than they have made, and taken more than they have given. They have made a life, but not a difference, and that disappointment and regret haunts their soul. We strive to make a difference because we realize we have not.

The world cannot wait for the final chapter to be written before its people contribute their unique talents to the betterment of its future. Take a chance to make a change, and make a change to make a difference. You will achieve your destiny.

We seek to change because we seek to make a difference, and without a chance, rarely can that difference be made. Once presented with that opportunity, you must have the determination to risk all for the hope of something better. That something better is an idea whose time has come, an idea pursued with a great sense of confidence in its outcome. That is how change can illuminate a better way and a better future.

Take a chance to make a change,
and make a change to make a difference.

CHAPTER 8
The Great Changes for Our Age

In theory, change is quite simplistic; in practice, it can become quite convoluted. There are reasons why we should seek change. In general, change is sought to improve upon the situation that exists today and to create a more advantageous and prosperous future.

The process of change, or how change should occur, should be straightforward and methodical. In general, the process demands we research where we need to go and galvanize our resources toward that ambition.

Finally, there are certain traits and circumstances that are needed for change to have the best opportunity to succeed. Change is rarely achieved in any other manner than by passionate and driven people pursuing righteous and just ambitions.

> We have learned why change should occur, how change can be accomplished, and what traits and circumstances are vital to achieving change. What is often most contentious is what type of change should occur. What are the righteous and just ambitions that should be the focus of our efforts to change the world in which we live? Universal concurrence and agreement can never be achieved, but I believe there are three specific aspects of our world and its society that should be addressed and changed to advance the interests of the world and better the future of its people. They are from irresponsibility to responsibility, from destruction to construction, and from unkind to kind.

From irresponsibility to responsibility
The most deplorable trait among so many in our society is the inability or unwillingness to take responsibility for the life in which you live. Too many seek far and wide for someone to blame or search to find any excuse that can serve as the reason for the failures that have befallen their life. Others rarely are the source of our failure or the cause of our troubles. Rather, it is the damaging choices we have made and the inevitable consequences that follow that frame the disappointments and dejection that are so common as our years progress.

There always seems to be someone to blame for one's lot in life. Back in the day, we were taught that you reaped what you sowed, you got what you deserved, and the only person you can blame is yourself. Today, the nearly universal claims are that "you were tricked," "someone took advantage of you," "you were treated unfairly," or "it is not fair." Rare is the individual who is accountable for his or her actions and takes responsibility for the destructive choices he or she has made throughout life. Oh, how far we have fallen.

Irresponsible conduct leads to predictable consequences. That consequence is failure, and the cause of that failure can be traced back to irresponsibility. The truth is that we have far more power to control our future than others do to destroy it. We have the ability to study more, save more, invest more, exercise more, and work more. We have the strength to waste less, drink less, smoke less, and sin less. And finally, we have the capacity to restrain our ego, jealousy, and envy.

The United States was created in the mold of the rugged individual, a person who could create his or her own life without unnecessary and undue influence from the government. Though there are exceptions, that same logic holds true today. Success can be achieved by having the right idea, taking a risk, sacrificing your time and enjoyments, working hard, having some luck, and having some help. There are disappointments along the way, to be sure, but failure as a result of hard work and sacrifice are inconceivable over the long term.

Take ownership of the choices that have created the life in which you live, and recognize that the choices you make today allow you to change the path of your life. Take that opportunity, assume responsibility for what you do and who you become, and live your life according to your own compass. It will be a more satisfying life and a more satisfied society, as all strive to achieve their own ambitions rather than that of their neighbors. Their future will become their own.

We can live a more peaceful and productive life, if only we have the determination to take that chance and assume the responsibility that once defined the American spirit.

From destruction to construction

In the first half of the twentieth century, the United States was an ascending nation. By the end of that century, it had fallen precipitously from its lofty perch. Where citizens once felt the euphoria of a rising standard of living—plentiful jobs, company-paid health care and retirement, and an ever-increasing potpourri of government benefits—Americans today feel the sand slipping through their fingers. Benefits and government services are too expensive to maintain, jobs are moving overseas or becoming irrelevant through technology, and our nation's infrastructure is decaying. The United States does not seem to build much anymore, concentrating instead on tearing apart buildings and society alike.

There seems to be greater interest in being an uncommon individual rather than a common citizen, which can be a destructive path for a country that survives on a shared culture. The United States could never afford the number of police officers needed if its people did not voluntarily follow the nation's law. This country has progressed, and its people prospered, because nearly all believe in the principles of its shared culture—that you obey the laws and pay your taxes, that you work hard and keep most of what you earn, that you share with those who are less fortunate, and that in some way you work to make the world a better place. That belief seems to have frayed over the decades, but it can be changed.

A sea change in thought is needed throughout this country. Americans must spend more time and effort constructing and restructuring the basic building block of society. The rush to denigrate and degrade the government, Fortune 500 businesses, the rich and the poor, management and unions, the unemployed, Republicans and Democrats, races and nationalities, other countries, and multinational corporations must cease.

Rarely has the wanton destruction of someone or something else resulted in a safer and more secure future. Instead, such ambitions result only in advancing the interests of one person at the expense of another. Over time, such conduct would destroy the bonds of citizenship throughout this country, forsaking that which is best for our country for that which is best for one citizen.

This country was founded on the principles of work and sacrifice, equality and justice, and unity not division. Though not all have benefited equally, through two centuries, Americans perfected these ideals to create a more fair and giving country. Sadly, economic challenges, political miscalculations, and societal selfishness have dimmed the luster of these ideals.

Without reservation, we can change the destructive path of this country. What has been destroyed can be rebuilt, and future generations can have the chance at a better life. The ideals that once created a society that was the envy of the world can do so again, but only through painful sacrifices, hard work, and a commitment to helping your fellow man. It can be done, and for the future of our country, it must be done.

From unkind to kind

In my family, I was taught two important lessons. I imparted them and another onto my children. They were:

- My grandmother Vee McCoy believed that one should pass and repass and never let the negative comments or conduct of others affect the manner in which you live or treat others.

- My parents, John and Mary Gualco, believed their children should control their attitude, emotions, and personality and never let anyone alter the foundations of a decent and honorable person that the family strived to develop in each succeeding generation.

- I taught my children, Gunner and Toria, to always look for the good along the road of life and never let jealousy, envy, negativity, or unhappiness affect your positive outlook and enthusiasm for living a truly remarkable life.

- At the heart of these lessons is the concept of kindness. I remain stunned at the general rudeness that pervades so much of our everyday life. We witness the Machiavellian efforts of some coworkers to impact our career. We must drive defensively and cautiously because of the aggressive and unsafe nature of others. We are taught to not help those stranded on the roadways or talk to fellow riders on the subway because we cannot predict their response. We cannot compliment the beauty of some or offer constructive advice to others for fear of offending their psyche. Our doors are locked, our windows are barred, and we have moved to gated communities to offer a modicum of safety to our family. Armed guards are posted at movie theaters, restaurants, hotels, grocery stores, parking lots, and schools. There are rows of cement barriers around many government buildings, and we spend hours to board a plane. We live in an era of great sensitivity, struggle, and danger. It seems to have gone so wrong, so fast.

Most unfortunate, the common decencies seem to be fading from our society. Fewer call their elders Mr. or Mrs. Fewer offer their seat when an elderly person enters a crowded subway, and few allow customers with just a couple of items in their grocery cart to move ahead in line. Even a friendly greeting seems to be a rarity these days as we listen to our iPods.

It has been a monumental shift in attitudes and conduct within this country over the past generation or two. Being rude seems more common and more tolerated than ever before, and being kind has become more of an aberration. It is a true travesty. But just as rudeness has become commonplace, kindness can be resurrected.

We all can learn to be more grateful for our good fortune and less ungrateful for our challenges. We can learn to take less and give more, and we can learn to care more for the happiness of others and care less for our own selfish pursuits. We can learn to be kind again, and, in doing so, we can change the very fabric of a country that was once great and can be great again.

In a world that demands monumental change, we are limited only by our dreams of a better world and the determination to make a difference. We can create a world where people are grateful for what they have and not ungrateful for what they do not have, who give more than they take, who assume responsibility for their actions and don't seek blame as an excuse, and who work to rebuild our planet rather than destroying its natural resources.

We can do something to make the world a better place, and we can contribute to the betterment of mankind. Most important of all, our life on earth will have made a difference, which is the eternal ambition and crowning achievement of a decent and honorable life.

Change is achieved by passionate and driven people pursuing righteous and just ambitions.

Appendix
The Story of the Backpack

I believe that when we are born, we are given a backpack
with certain traits, characteristics, talents,
and advantages.
We then spend the remaining moments of
our life perfecting those traits,
characteristics, talents, and advantages.

We should live every day using those blessings to do
something great with our time so that, upon its end,
we can return the backpack and say:

That you fought the good fight,
that you did the best you could with what you had,
that you did the right thing for the right reason,
and that, in some small way,
you made the world a better place.

It is the reason I carry a backpack every day of my life.

Do Something Good

Do something good.

If you spend your time doing good,

maybe the Good Lord will let you stick around a bit longer.